Elegant Desserts

JUNE ROTH

Elegant Desserts

DODD, MEAD & COMPANY
New York

*To my husband Fred,
with deep appreciation of his unselfish
foresight, unwavering encouragement, and
uncompromising sense of good taste*

Contents

1 

Dessert Showmanship

An elegant dessert can create a food memory that lingers long after the last crumbs are brushed away—if you have taken the care to serve it with flair!

Every experienced and successful hostess knows that her reputation as a good cook depends on recipes that are unusually delicious and reliable. This book is a treasury of such recipes to make your dessert course a special event. Lavish ingredients are used with shapely molds, crystal bowls, footed cake stands, and some special equipment to make it all possible. Here and there you will find a sleight-of-hand recipe that is labeled "a dietetic dessert" or "a quick-trick way" for those moments of counting calories or using convenience food head starts. All have been chosen for taste and appearance—to make your dessert course a pleasing endeavor.

To help you create and show off these desserts in a way that will emphasize their elegance, here are utensils and accessories to consider:

ROUND CAKE STANDS OR PLATTERS in china, crystal, or silver. They come in varying heights and sizes to display molded desserts, cakes, tortes, and open pies to their best advantage.

LARGE COMPOTES in china, crystal, or silver. Fruit and puddings assume extra graciousness when served from a footed compote. Sometimes these are available with individual serving dishes to match, so that ladling each serving of dessert becomes part of the tasteful experience.

CAKE STAND

COMPOTE

SMALL CRYSTAL BOWL for fruit, puddings, and profiteroles, when you are serving fewer people and want the see-through glamour of crystal.

LARGE DEEP-BOWL for trifles. This can be of crystal or of thin modern glass. The beauty of a trifle is the intriguing glimpse of its mutiple ingredients through the sides of the bowl.

A TIERED PLATTER in china, crystal, or silver is delightful for serving cookies, tartlets, and small pickup cakes. A triple graduated tier in particular will lend an aura of importance to the serving of finger food.

MOLDS for the shaping of mousses, Bavarians, charlottes, bombes, and gelatin desserts. They are available in all sizes and shapes. It does not matter whether they are made of metal, glass, china, or plastic unless they

TIERED PLATTER

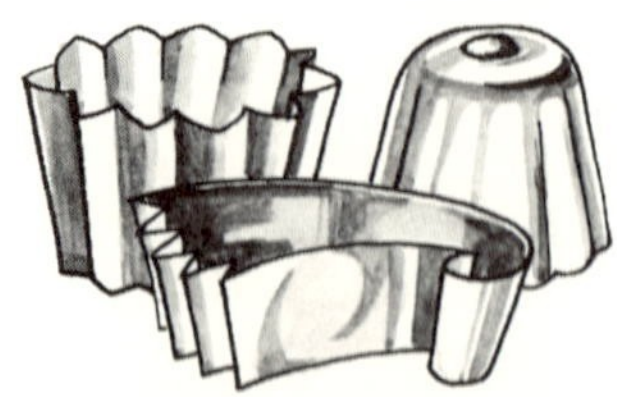

MOLDS

will also be used for kitchen ornamentation. Covered molds, necessary for steamed puddings, can be found in imported kitchenware departments.

STEAM PUDDING MOLD with a tight-fitting lid if you plan to prepare any of these bake-and-steam desserts. These are usually imported and may be found in gourmet kitchenware departments.

POTS DE CRÈME made of china are available in individual serving size

STEAM PUDDING MOLD

POTS DE CRÈME

for single portions of mousse or pudding. These often have lids and saucers and can go from refrigerator to table with ease.

CAKE PANS, including different-sized layer cake pans, spring forms, bundt pans, angel food rings, and jelly roll pans. Heavy, shiny, seamfree aluminum is your best choice, with special linings a matter of preference. The greater the variety of pans you can acquire, the greater your versatility in serving dessert.

PIE PLATES of several sizes, including scalloped-edged flan pans and straight-rimmed tart pans. These may be of metal or ovenproof glass, and occasionally of ovenware ceramic too.

SPRING FORM

BUNDT PAN

SOUFFLÉ DISH

FLAN PAN

SOUFFLÉ DISHES of varying sizes are made of ovenware ceramic, many with handsome colorings for oven-to-table use. They always have straight sides and should be ungreased (unless otherwise indicated) to enable the egg mixtures to climb the walls of the dish.

TARTLET PAN

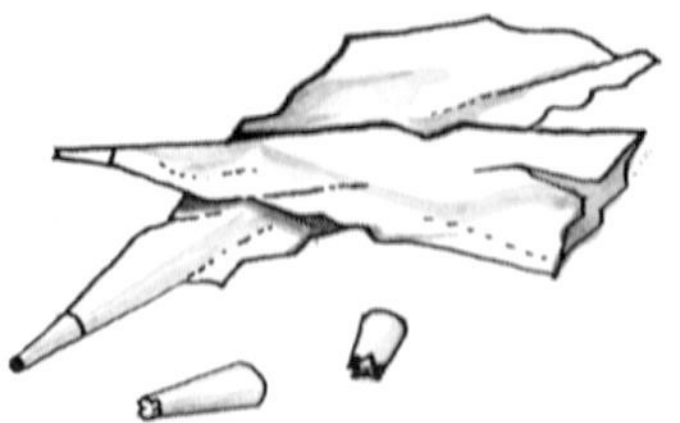

PASTRY BAG

Cookie sheets and tartlet pans for the making of small desserts. Shiny seamless aluminum is the easiest to clean, unless you prefer specially lined ovenware. Tartlet pans are available in many shapes and sizes at gourmet kitchenware shops or restaurant supply stores.

An electric mixer of large capacity will enable you to prepare many recipes with ease. Extra bowls are an asset for beating eggs separately. A dough hook attachment makes kneading a simple chore. Small electric hand mixers are also useful for some beating procedures.

A blender will grind nuts, purée fruits, and find many other uses in your kitchen. The more speeds your blender has, the greater your versatility in using it.

A pastry bag with a variety of tips is essential if you intend to pipe icing or whipped cream for elaborate creations. A little practice will turn you into an enthusiastic user. If you prefer, you may obtain a well-made aluminum cookie press with extra tips for decorating as well—a plunger at one end makes it easy to handle.

Before attempting to prepare any recipe, read it through carefully to evaluate the ingredients, utensils, and time you will need to make that dessert. Although all the recipes are intended for the average homemaker in a moderately equipped kitchen, some are more difficult to assemble than others. Many of these are from famous European pastry chefs who generously gave of their time to explain their procedures in detail as I worked with them to develop these recipes for your kitchen.

When choosing a dessert to be the *pièce de résistance* of a dinner party, consider the menu as a whole. If the main course is hot and heavy, perhaps something cold and fluffy is in order. If the entire meal is rather lightweight, a cake or torte will balance it. Plan a menu as an artist plans a balanced painting, for you, too, are dealing with a creative art form—one that has color, texture, temperature, and taste. All of these appeal to the senses, and when combined with a little extra showmanship, can make dessert a flourishing finish to a fine dinner.

2

Luxurious Mousses, Bavarians, and Charlottes

For sheer beauty and palate pleasure, some of the most impressive kinds of desserts are to be found among these molded offerings. Surprisingly, they are among the easiest of recipes to follow and will evoke the most "oohs and aahs" from your guests.

You can differentiate among the three varieties if you know the simple factors that distinguish each one:

A MOUSSE is a frothy mixture usually based on separated eggs or whipped cream, or a combination of both. It may be made in a molded form, served from individual pots de crème, or spooned into individual serving dishes from a large bowl in which it was chilled.

A BAVARIAN usually starts with an egg custard base, sometimes mixed with whipped cream, and always has gelatin to hold it together. It is often flavored with liqueur, fruit, chocolate, or nuts.

A CHARLOTTE always has a framework of ladyfingers or bread slices holding a sweet filling of custard or fruit.

All three are served chilled and can be decorated with whipped cream or fruit. Despite their rich ingredients they are among the lightest of all desserts. It is possible to become renowned as a fabulous dessert-maker, without knowing a thing about baking, if you learn to prepare these delectable creations.

TAFFY RUM MOUSSE

Rum and molasses, suspended in whipped cream, make this recipe a guest sensation. Picture the palate searchers as they try to identify the elusive taste:

TAFFY RUM MOUSSE

    2 envelopes (2 tablespoons) unflavored gelatin
    1 cup cold water
    ½ cup sugar
    ½ cup unsulphured molasses
    ¾ cup light rum
    ½ cup milk
    2 cups heavy cream, whipped
       chopped pistachio nuts, optional

Sprinkle gelatin over water in medium saucepan. Place over low heat; stir constantly until gelatin dissolves, about 3 minutes. Remove from heat; add sugar and stir until dissolved. Stir in molasses and rum. Add milk. Chill, stirring occasionally, until consistency of unbeaten egg white. Fold in whipped cream. Turn into a 2-quart mold; chill until firm, about 3 or 4 hours, or place in freezer for 2 hours. Unmold. If desired, garnish with additional whipped cream and chopped pistachio nuts. Makes 10 servings.

APRICOT-PECAN MOUSSE

1   3-ounce package lemon gelatin
1   cup boiling water
1   1-pound can apricot halves
2   tablespoons apricot brandy
2   cups heavy cream, whipped
½   cup chopped pecan nuts

Combine lemon gelatin with boiling water; stir until completely dissolved. Drain ½ cup juice from can of apricot halves; stir into gelatin mixture. Add apricot brandy. Pour remaining contents of apricots, including the rest of juice, into an electric blender; purée very fine. Stir into gelatin mixture. Chill until mixture has the consistency of egg whites, then remove from refrigerator and fold in whipped cream and chopped pecans. Pour into a 6-cup mold and chill until firm. Unmold and serve with additional whipped cream, if desired. Makes 6 to 8 servings.

ALMOND MOUSSE

    2 egg whites
  2½ cups finely ground almonds
    1 cup sugar
    8 egg whites beaten stiff
  12 ounces Baker's German sweet chocolate
    1 quart fresh strawberries, washed and hulled
    2 tablespoons curaçao
       candied violets
       walnut halves

Stir 2 egg whites, ground almonds, and sugar together in a heavy saucepan; heat until warmed through and the consistency of a thick mush. Cool. Fold into stiffly beaten egg whites. Pour into a well-greased 1½-quart circular ring mold; place the ring mold in a pan of water. Bake at 350°F. for 30 to 35 minutes. Remove from oven and cool for about 10 minutes. Then chill. When cold, melt chocolate in the top of a double boiler, over boiling water. Paint chocolate over the mousse with a pastry brush and smooth with a spatula; the chocolate should be just a thin, smooth covering. Fill center of the mousse with fresh strawberries, sprinkle with curaçao. Decorate with candied violets and walnut halves placed attractively on top of the chocolate. Makes 12 servings.

CHOCOLATE PRUNE MOUSSE
(A Quick-trick Way)

  1 cup slivered, pitted prunes
 ½ cup brandy or orange juice
  2 3⅝-ounce packages chocolate pudding mix
  3 cups milk
  1 cup heavy cream

Snip prunes with scissors and soak in brandy or orange juice one hour or longer. Prepare pudding as directed on package (except, use 1½ cups milk per package). Drain prunes and add to pudding. Chill. Whip cream and fold gently into pudding, with remaining liquor (up to 4 table-spoons). Turn into serving bowl or small pots. Cover and refrigerate. To serve, decorate with strips of prune or a star of whipped cream centered with a brandied prune. Makes 12 servings.

While this dessert is designed for individual pots de crème, it may also be spooned at the table from a large glass compote. It's a sweet treat, either way.

CHOCOLATE MOUSSE CUPS

1 8-ounce sweet chocolate candy bar (of fine quality)
4 tablespoons butter, softened
¼ cup heavy cream
1 tablespoon sugar
1 teaspoon brandy
5 egg whites
¼ cup heavy cream, whipped

Melt chocolate in the top of a double boiler, over hot water. Remove from heat and mix thoroughly with bits of butter, until smooth. Stir in cream and sugar. Stir in brandy. Cool to room temperature. Beat egg whites stiff; fold in chocolate mixture. Pour into individual pots de crème. Chill. Top with a dollop of whipped cream before serving. Makes 6 servings.

This Cherry Heering Mousse, and the Almond Mousse on page 8 were part of a fabulous dessert buffet prepared by Jorgen Ramstedt, head chef of the Sheraton-Copenhagen Hotel, when I was recently guest of honor of the Hotel and Restaurant Managers' Association of Denmark. It was an evening I shall never forget, and it pleases me to bring these recipes to you from my dear friends in Denmark.

CHERRY HEERING MOUSSE

¾ cup Cherry Heering liqueur
3 envelopes (3 tablespoons) unflavored gelatin
1 teaspoon lemon juice
2 tablespoons cherry jam
½ cup sugar
8 egg yolks
1 quart heavy cream, whipped
   macaroons, optional

STRAWBERRY MOUSSE

Into a small saucepan, pour ½ cup of the liqueur, ½ envelope of the gelatin, and the lemon juice; stir until gelatin is dissolved. Then heat and stir briskly to dissolve it completely. Pour this mixture into a 2-quart mold and chill. Using the same saucepan, pour the remaining ¼ cup of liqueur, the remaining 2½ envelopes of gelatin and the cherry jam into it; stir until gelatin is dissolved and then heat until mixture is smooth except for cherries in the jam. Stir in sugar, and mix until dissolved. Set aside to cool at room temperature. Beat egg yolks until thick and fluffy; slowly beat in this last mixture. Fold in stiffly beaten whipped cream. Remove mold from the refrigerator and add this filling. Chill for several hours. To serve, unmold and garnish around the platter with macaroons. Makes 8 to 10 servings.

STRAWBERRY MOUSSE

> 1 *pint strawberries, sliced*
> ½ *cup sugar*
>   *water*
> 1 *3-ounce package strawberry flavor gelatin*
> 1 *pint strawberry ice cream*
> ½ *cup flaked coconut*
> ½ *cup finely chopped pecans*
>   *sweetened sliced strawberries*

In a bowl toss strawberries and sugar; let stand at room temperature at least one hour, tossing occasionally; drain and reserve juice. Add sufficient water to strawberry juice to make 1 cup. Bring liquid to boiling. In a bowl pour boiling liquid over gelatin; stir until dissolved. Spoon ice cream into hot gelatin mixture; stir until melted. Cool. When partially thickened, whip in a mixing bowl at highest speed for about 2 minutes. Fold in strawberries, coconut, and pecans. Arrange reserved sweetened strawberries in bottom of 4-cup mold to conform to design. Turn mixture into mold; chill until firm. Garnish with additional strawberries. Makes 6 to 8 servings.

Here's a perfect answer to your problem of dessert for a dieting guest! It looks rich, creamy, and forbidden, but turns out to be sugar- and fat-free, with an unbelievable easy-in-the-blender technique.

PUMPKIN-PINEAPPLE MOUSSE
(A Diet Dessert)

2 envelopes (2 tablespoons) unflavored gelatin
½ cup cold water
¾ cup boiling water
⅔ cup nonfat dry milk solids
2 teaspoons liquid nonnutritive sweetener
½ teaspoon cinnamon
¼ teaspoon nutmeg
½ teaspoon salt
2 tablespoons lemon juice
1 cup canned or cooked pumpkin
1 8½-ounce can dietetic-packed pineapple tidbits, drained
8 ice cubes

Sprinkle gelatin over cold water in a 5-cup blender container; allow to soften while assembling other ingredients. Pour boiling water into blender. Cover. Process at low speed until gelatin is dissolved. If gelatin granules cling to container, use a rubber spatula to push them into mixture. Add nonfat dry milk, sweetener, cinnamon, nutmeg, salt, and lemon juice. Process at low speed until well blended. Add pumpkin and pineapple. Process at low, then high speed, until well blended. Add ice cubes, one at a time, and process at high speed until ice is melted. Pour into sherbet glasses and chill. Makes 6 servings.

PUMPKIN-PINEAPPLE MOUSSE

COFFEE MOUSSE AND STRAWBERRIES

> 1 envelope (1 tablespoon) unflavored gelatin
> 1 cup water
> ¾ cup extra strong coffee
> 2 tablespoons sugar
> 1 cup heavy cream, whipped
> 1 pint fresh strawberries, sliced
> 2 tablespoons confectioners' sugar

In a saucepan, soften gelatin in water; then heat and stir until gelatin is completely dissolved. Remove from heat, stir in coffee and sugar. Refrigerate until mixture mounds slightly when dropped from a spoon. Fold in whipped cream. Pour into a 1-quart serving dish or compote. Chill until set. Meanwhile, combine strawberries and 1 tablespoon of sifted confectioners' sugar; place over top of chilled mousse and sift remaining confectioners' sugar over berries. Makes 6 servings.

COFFEE MOUSSE AND STRAWBERRIES

VANILLA BAVARIAN WITH BLUEBERRY SAUCE

2 envelopes (2 tablespoons) unflavored gelatin
4 tablespoons water
¾ cup sugar
1 teaspoon vanilla
12 egg yolks
1 quart heavy cream

Soften gelatin in 2 tablespoons of the water; set aside. Place the remaining 2 tablespoons of water, the sugar and vanilla in the top section of a double boiler; place over direct heat and stir until mixture comes to a boil. Remove from heat. Beat egg yolks well and pour into sugar mixture; place over simmering water in lower half of double boiler and return to heat, beating constantly. Stir in softened gelatin and mix until dissolved. Remove from heat and cool. Whip cream. Fold cooled mixture with whipped cream. Pour into a 2-quart mold and chill until set. Unmold when ready to serve, and pass the Blueberry Sauce. Makes 12 servings.

BLUEBERRY SAUCE:
1 cup blueberries
½ cup water
⅓ cup sugar
1 teaspoon cornstarch
⅛ teaspoon salt
1 teaspoon butter
2 tablespoons lemon juice

Boil half the blueberries in the water for about 3 minutes. Mix together the sugar, cornstarch, and salt, and stir into hot berries. Cook and stir until thickened and clear. Add remaining berries and simmer for a few minutes. Stir in butter and lemon juice. Chill. Serve with Vanilla Bavarian.

This recipe follows the classic technique, using egg yolks, hot milk, sugar, gelatin, and whipped cream. The gelatin helps to hold the delicate cream mixture high and firm as it chills. Treat your taste buds to the exquisite combination of warm sauce over this molded dessert.

GOLDEN BAVARIAN

  1 *envelope (1 tablespoon) unflavored gelatin*
  2 *tablespoons cold water*
  4 *egg yolks*
  ½ *cup sugar*
  1 *cup hot milk*
  ½ *teaspoon vanilla*
  1 *cup heavy cream, whipped*
  ½ *cup anise-flavored liqueur (Galliano)*
  1 *16-ounce can whole apricots, drained*

Soften gelatin in cold water. In top of a double boiler, beat together egg yolks and sugar until very thick. Gradually stir in milk, then vanilla. Cook over simmering water, stirring constantly, until thickened and smooth. Add softened gelatin; stir until dissolved. Cool, stirring occasionally, until slightly thickened. Fold in cream and liqueur. Pour into a 1-quart mold and chill until set, about 4 hours. Unmold and garnish with apricots. Serve with Golden Fruit Sauce. Makes 6 servings.

    GOLDEN FRUIT SAUCE:
  1 *cup pineapple juice*
  ¼ *cup sugar*
    juice of half a lemon
  1 *tablespoon cornstarch*
  2 *tablespoons undiluted frozen orange juice concentrate*
  ¼ *cup anise-flavored liqueur (Galliano)*

Mix pineapple juice with sugar and lemon juice in a saucepan; bring to a boil. Blend cornstarch with undiluted frozen orange juice concentrate; stir into boiling mixture. Cook, stirring constantly, until slightly thickened and clear. Stir in liqueur. Serve warm, not hot.

GOLDEN BAVARIAN

EGGNOG BAVARIAN

EGGNOG BAVARIAN

3 envelopes (3 tablespoons) unflavored gelatin
¾ cup cold water
4 cups dairy eggnog
¼ cup sugar
¼ teaspoon nutmeg
1 cup heavy cream, whipped

Sprinkle gelatin on water to soften. In a 2-quart saucepan place 1 cup eggnog, sugar, nutmeg, and softened gelatin. Heat over low heat, stirring occasionally, until gelatin is dissolved. Add remaining 3 cups eggnog; chill until partially set. Fold in whipped cream; turn into 7-cup mold. Chill until firm. Unmold and serve with Winter Sauce. Makes 12 servings.

WINTER SAUCE:

¾ cup sugar
½ cup water
1 cup cranberries
¼ cup water
½ teaspoon unflavored gelatin
1 cup chopped apple
⅓ cup chopped walnuts

In 1½-quart saucepan combine sugar and ½ cup water; bring to a boil. Add cranberries and boil 5 minutes. Meanwhile, soften gelatin in ¼ cup water; add to cranberry mixture and stir until dissolved. Remove from heat; add apple and walnuts. Cool. Serve with Eggnog Bavarian. Makes about 2 cups.

MOCHA CHARLOTTE

1 6-ounce package semisweet chocolate morsels
2 tablespoons strong coffee
4 eggs, separated
½ teaspoon vanilla
18 ladyfingers, split
1 cup heavy cream, whipped

Melt chocolate and coffee together in the top of a double boiler, over hot water. Remove from heat. Cool slightly. Beat egg yolks into chocolate mixture, one at a time. Add vanilla. Beat egg whites stiff. Fold in chocolate mixture. Line sides and bottom of a 1-quart mold with split ladyfingers, cut side facing in. Pour in half of the chocolate mixture. Cover with a layer of ladyfingers; add remaining mixture and top with ladyfingers, cut side down. Cover with plastic wrap and chill for several hours. Unmold and cover top with whipped cream, decorating with a pastry bag, if desired. Makes 8 servings.

According to culinary history, in the nineteenth century the great French chef Carême, who cooked for the royal households of England, Austria, and Russia, created the Charlotte Russe. This jellied custard set in a crown of ladyfingers was thought to be named for Princess Charlotte of England, although made for the Czar of Russia. You'll find that it has a royal taste.

CHARLOTTE RUSSE

24 *single ladyfingers (approximately)*
 2 *envelopes (2 tablespoons) unflavored gelatin*
¼ *cup cold water*
¼ *cup boiling water*
 1 *cup sugar*
 3 *tablespoons lemon juice*
½ *cup orange liqueur (curaçao)*
½ *cup orange juice*
 3 *egg whites*
 1 *cup heavy cream, whipped*

Arrange ladyfingers around the sides of a 2-quart straight-sided mold. Soften gelatin in cold water, in a saucepan. Then add boiling water and stir until dissolved. Stir in sugar, lemon juice, orange liqueur, and orange juice. Heat and stir until mixture is free from granules. Cool at room temperature. Beat egg whites until stiff but not dry. Fold into the cooled gelatin mixture. Fold in whipped cream. Pour into prepared mold. Chill for several hours until firm. To serve, unmold and decorate with additional whipped cream, if desired. Makes 8 to 10 servings.

This will bring gasps of delight with every bite, even from your guests who may not like pumpkin pie. For the airiest results, be sure to chill the pumpkin mixture before combining with egg whites. It is a favorite dessert at Chez Roth.

PUMPKIN-SHERRY CHARLOTTE

  9 eggs, separated
1½ cups sugar
  3 cups canned pumpkin
1½ cups light cream
  2 teaspoons cinnamon
  1 teaspoon nutmeg
 ¼ teaspoon ginger
 ½ teaspoon salt
  3 envelopes (3 tablespoons) unflavored gelatin
1½ cups sweet sherry
  6 tablespoons butter
  1 tablespoon vanilla
12 ladyfingers, split
 ½ cup heavy cream, whipped

In a large saucepan, beat egg yolks until lemony, then beat in sugar. Add pumpkin, cream, cinnamon, nutmeg, ginger, and salt. Cook over very low heat, stirring constantly, until mixture thickens. Soften gelatin in sherry; stir into hot pumpkin mixture. Blend in butter and vanilla. Chill until mixture thickens. Beat egg whites until stiff; fold into pumpkin mixture. Arrange split ladyfingers, cut side in, around the sides of a 10-inch spring form. Pour in pumpkin mixture. Chill for several hours. When ready to serve, remove side of spring form and decorate top with whipped cream. Makes 12 to 14 servings.

PINEAPPLE CHARLOTTE

 1 20-ounce can crushed pineapple
    water
 1 envelope (1 tablespoon) unflavored gelatin
 ½ cup sugar
 ⅛ teaspoon salt
 1 cup heavy cream
12 ladyfingers, split
    whipped cream, optional
    pecans, optional

Drain syrup from pineapple into measuring cup; add water to make 1 cup. Sprinkle gelatin over syrup mixture in medium saucepan. Place over low heat; stir constantly until gelatin dissolves, 2 to 3 minutes. Remove from heat; stir in sugar and salt. Add pineapple. Chill, stirring occasionally, until mixture mounds slightly when dropped from spoon. Whip cream; fold into pineapple mixture. Line sides of a 6-cup mold with split ladyfingers. Turn pineapple mixture into mold. Chill until firm. Unmold on serving platter. Garnish with additional whipped cream and pecans, if desired. Makes 6 to 8 servings.

PINEAPPLE CHARLOTTE

ORANGE CHARLOTTE

> 1 envelope (1 tablespoon) unflavored gelatin
> ½ cup sugar
> ⅛ teaspoon salt
> 2 eggs, separated
> 1¼ cups orange juice
> 2 teaspoons grated orange rind
> 12 ladyfingers, split
> 1 cup heavy cream, whipped
> 2 oranges, peeled and sectioned

Combine gelatin, ¼ cup of the sugar, and salt in top of double boiler. Beat egg yolks slightly and add with orange juice to gelatin mixture. Cook over boiling water, stirring until gelatin dissolves and mixture thickens slightly, about 8 minutes. Remove from heat; stir in rind. Chill until mixture is slightly thicker than consistency of unbeaten egg white. While mixture is chilling, line an 8- by 4-inch loaf pan with wax paper, letting ends extend beyond rim of pan. Line bottom and sides of pan with ladyfinger halves. Beat egg whites until soft peaks form; gradually add remaining ¼ cup sugar and beat until very stiff. Fold into gelatin mixture. Fold in whipped cream. Turn mixture into prepared pan. Chill until firm, 6 hours or overnight. Lift out of pan to serving dish; remove paper. Garnish with orange sections and whipped cream or whipped topping, if desired. Makes 6 to 8 servings.

3

Delicate Puddings, Crèmes, and Flans

There are times when a cold and creamy-textured dessert can satisfy a sweet tooth best. It may be served from one large bowl or pot into individual servings from the start. Parfait glasses and footed glasses are fine for single portions when you want to present them in an important way.

Most puddings are cooked and chilled, while others are baked in a greased, covered tin especially made for this purpose. Sometimes you will note directions for setting the pan in water while it bakes, known in culinary circles as a "water bath." These baked puddings and crèmes will hold their shape when removed from their pans, while the boiled counterparts need a supporting rim and must be spooned for serving.

The basic ingredients for puddings and crèmes are eggs, milk, sugar, a thickening agent, and a flavoring. This presents a heavier, creamier texture than the frothy desserts of the mousse, Bavarian, and charlotte varieties. Consider them, therefore, as a closing touch to an otherwise lightweight dinner, to give a feeling of sweet, satisfying fulfillment.

There are many variations of this Italian custard, but this is the basic version used in Italy. It can be made at tableside with a chafing dish. It helps to have a master wrist beating with a good whisk too!

ZABAGLIONE

> 6 eggs
> ¼ cup confectioners' sugar
>   pinch of salt
> ⅓ cup Marsala wine

Put eggs, sugar, and salt in the top of a double boiler, over hot water. Cook and beat constantly for about 6 minutes, until mixture is very thick and light. Add the wine and beat again until mixture is very thick. Pour into stemmed dessert glasses (large wine glasses will do nicely for this) and serve at once. Or, if preferred, chill and serve several hours later. Makes 4 servings.

Here's an American version using electric equipment and plentiful oranges to produce a cool, smooth dessert. For a novelty, substitute Sabra (an Israeli liqueur with a chocolate-orange flavor) for the suggested orange liqueur!

ZABAGLIONE L'ORANGE

> 6 egg yolks
> 1 teaspoon grated orange rind
> ¾ cup orange juice
> ¼ cup sugar
> 2 tablespoons orange liqueur

In top of double boiler, combine egg yolks, orange rind, juice, and sugar. Let stand for 15 minutes. Place over boiling water and beat with an electric mixer or rotary beater for 10 minutes, until mixture has tripled in volume. Remove from boiling water and place top of double boiler in bowl of ice water. Continue beating until zabaglione has cooled to room temperature. Fold in orange liqueur. Serve plain as a dessert or as a sauce over sweetened orange sections. Makes 6 servings.

The brown sugar will caramelize under the broiler, giving this crème its unique flavor. Be sure to watch over it with care, or your topping will have a burnt taste!

CRÈME BRÛLÉE

1   *pint heavy cream*
1   *teaspoon sugar*
6   *egg yolks*
½   *teaspoon vanilla*
2   *tablespoons strained brown sugar*

Scald the cream. Add sugar. Beat egg yolks and slowly add cream mixture to the yolks. Add vanilla. Pour through a strainer into 6 individual custard dishes. Place custard dishes in a pan of hot water, covering the dishes halfway. Bake in a 350°F. oven for 45 minutes. Remove from oven and chill for several hours. Just before serving, scatter 1 teaspoon of strained brown sugar over the top of each custard cup; slip under the broiler and watch until the sugar turns dark brown. Remove and serve. Makes 6 servings.

BANANA CRÈME DE BRÛLÉE
(A Quick-trick Way)

> 1 package (4-serving size) banana cream pudding
> 1½ cups milk
> 1 teaspoon rum extract (optional)
> 2 cups whipped cream
> ⅓ cup firmly packed brown sugar
> ½ teaspoon ground cinnamon
> 2 ripe bananas

Prepare pudding with 1½ cups milk as directed on package. Cover surface with wax paper; chill. Beat pudding until smooth. Add rum extract. Blend whipped cream into pudding. Pour into heatproof 1-quart casserole. Mix brown sugar and cinnamon. Sprinkle over top of pudding. Place casserole in preheated broiler, about 6 inches from heat. Broil until sugar is bubbly and melted. Chill. Meanwhile slice bananas. Spoon pudding mixture over bananas in dessert dishes or use bananas as garnish. Makes about 3 cups of pudding or 6 servings.

BUTTERSCOTCH RICE PUDDING

> 1 3¾-ounce package butterscotch pudding and pie-filling
>   mix
> 1½ cups milk
> 2 eggs, separated
> 2 cups cooked rice
> 1 teaspoon vanilla
> 2 tablespoons brown sugar
>   Honey Sauce

Combine pudding mix, milk, and egg yolks. Cook over medium heat, stirring constantly, until thickened. Add rice and vanilla. Cool. Beat egg whites with brown sugar until whites stand in stiff peaks. Fold into pudding. Spoon into serving dishes. Chill. Top with Honey Sauce at serving time. Makes 6 servings.

HONEY SAUCE:

1 *cup heavy cream*
⅓ *cup honey*
1½ *teaspoons lemon juice*

Beat heavy cream until thick. Stir in honey and lemon juice.

APPLE PUDDING

½ *cup dark corn syrup*
 juice of 1 lemon
4 *large cooking apples, pared and thinly sliced (about 8 cups)*
½ *cup dairy sour cream*
½ *cup chopped walnuts or pecans*
¼ *cup confectioners' sugar*
 grated rind of 1 lemon
1 *cup heavy cream, whipped*

Combine corn syrup, lemon juice, and apples in 3-quart saucepan. Bring to boil over medium heat. Cover and simmer, stirring occasionally, until liquid is absorbed and apples are tender, about 30 minutes. Spoon into 1½-quart bowl. Chill. Combine sour cream, nuts, confectioners' sugar, and grated lemon rind. Fold into whipped cream. Spread over apple mixture. Chill. Makes 6 servings.

If you ever thought that rice pudding was dull family-fare, try it this way with bits of ginger snapping up the flavor. Serve it in low crystal bowls or high stemmed glasses for the most luxurious effect.

GINGER RICE PUDDING

- 1 cup dried figs
- 1 cup uncooked rice
- 1 cup water
- ½ teaspoon salt
- 2½ cups milk
- ½ cup honey
- 1 tablespoon butter
- 4 tablespoons finely minced preserved ginger
- ½ pint heavy cream, whipped

Cook figs in enough water to cover for about 30 minutes or until tender. Drain and chop fine. Combine rice, 1 cup water, and salt. Bring to a boil in top of double boiler. Cook 5 minutes. Add milk and return to a boil. Place over boiling water, cover, and continue cooking about 25 minutes, or until liquid is absorbed. Remove from heat. Stir in honey, butter, preserved ginger, and figs. Mix well. Chill. Fold in 1 cup of whipped cream. Spoon into dessert dishes and top with remaining cream. Makes 8 servings.

My request for a typical dessert recipe to charming Don Alfonso Font, director of the elegant Palace Hotel in Madrid, resulted in an immediate consultation with his head chef. Food Director Rafael F. de Bobadilla graciously translated as we worked to bring you this authentic delicate Spanish custard. Serve it with simple cake or cookies if you wish.

NATILLAS

4 cups milk
1 cup sugar
1 cinnamon stick, 4 inches long
3 tablespoons cornstarch
8 egg yolks
confectioners' sugar

In a heavy saucepan, stir milk and ¾ cup of the sugar together; add cinnamon stick. Bring to a boil. Remove from heat. In a bowl, combine remaining ¼ cup sugar with the cornstarch; stir in egg yolks until smooth. Stir egg yolk mixture slowly into hot milk mixture; return to heat and stir while mixture thickens. Do not allow to boil. Pour into 6 dessert bowls. Sprinkle lightly with confectioners' sugar. Serve cold.

Note: This custard pudding may also be poured into individual baking dishes and slipped under the broiler to lightly brown the confectioners' sugar. It is then served hot.

Pudding can take on extra glamour when served in alternating layers of a see-through parfait glass. Here are two pudding parfaits that are sure to please.

MOCHA PARFAIT

FIRST MIXTURE:
 1 *cup semisweet chocolate morsels*
 ⅓ *cup water*
 1 *tablespoon light corn syrup*
   dash salt
 2 *egg whites*
 ¼ *cup sugar*

Combine semisweet morsels, water, corn syrup, and salt and melt in top of double boiler over hot (not boiling) water. Let cool approximately 10 minutes. Beat egg whites until stiff but not dry. Add sugar gradually and beat until stiff and satiny. Fold egg white mixture into semisweet mixture.

SECOND MIXTURE:
 1 *cup heavy cream*
 1 *tablespoon instant coffee*
 ¼ *cup light brown sugar, firmly packed*
 ⅛ *teaspoon almond extract*

Combine all ingredients and beat until stiff. Spoon into parfait or sherbet glasses, alternating layers of semisweet chocolate mixture and coffee mixture. Chill well. Makes 6 to 8 servings.

CRANBERRY TAPIOCA PARFAITS

 1 *pound (4 cups) cranberries*
 3 *oranges, peeled and thinly sliced*
 3 *cups water*
 2 *cups sugar*
 6 *tablespoons quick-cooking tapioca*

MOCHA PARFAIT

1   *teaspoon grated orange rind*
½   *teaspoon ground cinnamon*
1   *cup heavy cream*
1   *to 2 tablespoons sugar*

Combine cranberries, orange slices, and water in saucepan. Cover and bring to a boil. Simmer until cranberry skins pop open. Press mixture through a sieve or a food grinder. Add 2 cups sugar, the tapioca, orange rind, and cinnamon; blend well. Return mixture to saucepan and bring to a boil. Then remove from heat, cover surface with wax paper, and chill thoroughly. Just before serving, whip cream with 1 to 2 tablespoons sugar. Stir chilled tapioca mixture. Spoon alternate layers of tapioca and whipped cream into parfait glasses. Makes 10 to 12 servings.

Following are a few chiffon creams of varying flavors. You'll love the fluffy texture—somewhere between a mousse and a pudding!

VANILLA CHIFFON CREAM

> 1 envelope (1 tablespoon) unflavored gelatin
> 2 tablespoons sugar
> ⅛ teaspoon salt
> 2 eggs, separated
> 2 cups milk
> 1½ teaspoons vanilla
> ¼ cup sugar

Mix together gelatin, 2 tablespoons sugar, and salt in a saucepan. Beat together egg yolks and milk; stir into gelatin mixture. Place over very low heat, stirring constantly, until gelatin dissolves (until there are no visible granules) and mixture thickens slightly, about 5 minutes. Remove from heat. Stir in vanilla. Chill, stirring occasionally, until mixture is thickened but not lumpy (until it mounds slightly when dropped from a spoon). Beat egg whites until soft peaks form; gradually add remaining sugar and beat until stiff. Fold gelatin mixture into beaten egg whites. Turn into 4-cup bowl, mold, or individual serving dishes. Chill until set. Makes 6 servings.

LEMON CHIFFON CREAM

> 1 envelope (1 tablespoon) unflavored gelatin
> 2 tablespoons sugar
> ⅛ teaspoon salt
> 2 eggs, separated
> 2 cups milk
> 2 teaspoons grated lemon rind
> 2 tablespoons lemon juice
> ¼ cup sugar

Mix together gelatin, 2 tablespoons sugar, and salt in a saucepan. Beat together egg yolks and milk; stir into gelatin mixture. Place over very low heat, stirring constantly, until gelatin dissolves (until there are no visible granules) and mixture thickens slightly, about 5 minutes. Remove from heat. Stir in grated lemon rind and lemon juice. Chill, stirring occasionally, until mixture is thickened but not lumpy (until it mounds slightly when dropped from a spoon). Beat egg whites until soft peaks form; gradually add remaining sugar and beat until stiff. Fold gelatin mixture into beaten egg whites. Turn into 4-cup bowl, mold, or individual serving dishes. Chill until set. Makes 6 servings.

CHOCOLATE CHIFFON CREAM

> 1 envelope (1 tablespoon) unflavored gelatin
> ¼ cup unsweetened cocoa
> 2 tablespoons sugar
> ⅛ teaspoon salt
> 2 eggs, separated
> 2 cups milk
> 1½ teaspoons vanilla
> ¼ cup sugar

Mix together gelatin, cocoa, 2 tablespoons sugar, and salt in a saucepan. Beat together egg yolks and milk; stir into gelatin mixture. Place over very low heat, stirring constantly, until gelatin dissolves (until there are no visible granules) and mixture thickens slightly, about 5 minutes. Remove from heat. Stir in vanilla. Chill, stirring occasionally, until mixture is thickened but not lumpy (until it mounds slightly when dropped from a spoon). Beat egg whites until soft peaks form; gradually add remaining sugar and beat until stiff. Fold gelatin mixture into beaten egg whites. Turn into 4-cup bowl, mold, or individual serving dishes. Chill until set. Makes 6 servings.

COFFEE CHIFFON CREAM

> 1 envelope (1 tablespoon) unflavored gelatin
> 2 tablespoons regular instant coffee powder
> 2 tablespoons sugar
> ⅛ teaspoon salt
> 2 eggs, separated
> 2 cups milk
> ½ teaspoon almond extract
> ¼ cup sugar

Mix together gelatin, 2 tablespoons sugar, instant coffee powder, and salt in a saucepan. Beat together egg yolks and milk; stir into gelatin mixture. Place over very low heat, stirring constantly, until gelatin dissolves (until there are no visible granules) and mixture thickens slightly, about 5 minutes. Remove from heat. Stir in almond extract. Chill, stirring occasionally, until mixture is thickened but not lumpy (until it mounds slightly when dropped from a spoon). Beat egg whites until soft peaks form; gradually add remaining sugar and beat until stiff. Fold gelatin mixture into beaten egg whites. Turn into 4-cup bowl, mold, or individual dishes. Chill until set. Makes 6 servings.

MAPLE-WALNUT CHIFFON CREAM

> 1 envelope (1 tablespoon) unflavored gelatin
> 2 cups milk
> ½ cup maple syrup
> ⅛ teaspoon salt
> 2 eggs, separated
> ½ cup chopped walnuts

Sprinkle gelatin over half of milk in saucepan; add ¼ cup syrup and salt. Beat egg yolks with remaining milk; stir into gelatin mixture. Place over very low heat, stirring constantly, until gelatin dissolves (until there are no visible granules) and mixture thickens slightly, about 5 minutes. Remove from heat. Chill, stirring occasionally, until mixture is thickened but not lumpy (until it mounds slightly when dropped from a spoon). Beat egg whites until soft peaks form; gradually add remaining ¼ cup syrup and beat until stiff. Fold gelatin mixture and chopped walnuts into beaten egg whites. Turn into 4-cup bowl, mold, or individual serving dishes. Chill until set. Makes 6 servings.

BAKED APPLE TAPIOCA

2 cups canned applesauce
⅓ cup brown sugar
2 teaspoons lemon juice
¼ teaspoon nutmeg
1 tablespoon butter
½ cup quick-cooking tapioca
1 quart milk
3 eggs, separated
⅓ cup sugar
¼ teaspoon salt
1 teaspoon vanilla
¼ teaspoon cream of tartar
½ cup sugar

Combine applesauce, brown sugar, lemon juice, and nutmeg. Place in 2½-quart casserole; dot with butter. Soak tapioca in 2 cups milk for 5 minutes. Beat egg yolks; add tapioca mixture, remaining 2 cups milk, ⅓ cup sugar, ¼ teaspoon salt, and vanilla extract. Pour over applesauce mixture. Bake in 325°F. oven for 75 minutes. Beat egg whites and cream of tartar until soft peaks form. Gradually beat in ½ cup sugar. Spread over tapioca. Bake an additional 15 minutes or until meringue is delicate brown. Serve cold. Makes 8 to 10 servings.

If your palate has not adjusted to cheese fondue, and you are wondering what to do with the fondue pot and forks, here's a delicious Chocolate Custard Fondue for an unusual fun-filled dessert.

CHOCOLATE CUSTARD FONDUE

  ½ cup cocoa
  ½ cup sugar
  ½ cup water
  4 eggs, slightly beaten
  ¼ teaspoon salt
  2 cups milk, scalded
  ½ teaspoon vanilla

In top of double boiler combine cocoa and sugar; gradually add water, stirring until smooth. Add eggs and salt; mix until well blended. Slowly pour milk into chocolate mixture, stirring constantly. Cook over simmering, not boiling, water, stirring constantly, until mixture just coats a silver spoon. Stir in vanilla. Pour into fondue pot; place on burner stand but do not light burner (mixture should stay hot while serving). If necessary to reheat, use low heat and stir constantly. Spear "dipper" with fondue fork and dip in sauce. Makes 6 to 8 servings.

Suggested "dippers": Angel food cake squares, pound cake squares, apple wedges, maraschino cherries, marshmallows, banana chunks.

GRAPE FOOL

 1½ pounds fresh grapes (4 cups)
  1 cinnamon stick
  ¼ teaspoon whole cloves
  ½ cup sugar
  2 teaspoons grated fresh orange rind
  1 cup heavy cream
 16 ladyfingers

Halve grapes and remove seeds. Combine with cinnamon, cloves, sugar, and orange rind in a saucepan and bring to a boil over medium heat, stirring constantly. Cook, uncovered, over low heat until grapes are reduced to a thick pulp, about 1½ hours. Stir frequently to prevent sticking. Remove whole spices and chill. Whip heavy cream until stiff and fold in grape pulp. Serve in dessert glasses lined with 2 ladyfingers each. Makes 8 servings.

ORANGE WHIP
(A Diet Dessert)

> 1 *envelope (1 tablespoon) unflavored gelatin*
> ½ *cup cold water*
> 1 *can (6 ounces) frozen orange juice concentrate, kept*
>   *frozen, divided*
>   *nonnutritive sweetener equivalent to ½ cup sugar*
> 2 *egg whites*
> ¼ *cup sugar*
> ½ *cup nonfat dry milk powder*
> ½ *cup ice water*

Sprinkle gelatin over water in saucepan. Place over low heat; stir constantly until gelatin dissolves, 2 to 3 minutes. Remove from heat. Reserve 1 tablespoon undiluted orange concentrate for beating with whipped milk; add the rest with nonnutritive sweetener to dissolved gelatin and stir until melted. Chill, stirring occasionally, until mixture thickens and mounds slightly when dropped from a spoon. Beat egg whites until soft peaks form. Gradually add sugar and beat until stiff peaks form; fold into orange mixture. In same mixing bowl combine dry milk powder and ice water. Using the same beater, beat until soft peaks form, 3 to 4 minutes. Add reserved 1 tablespoon undiluted orange concentrate. Continue beating until firm peaks form, 3 to 4 minutes longer. Fold into orange mixture. Spoon into small dessert dishes or demitasse cups, piling the mixture high. Refrigerate until set. Serve garnished, if desired, with mint sprigs and orange sections. Makes 12 servings, ½ cup each; 57 calories per serving.

These pie-shaped caramelized baked puddings are very popular in Europe and are often served with a bowl of whipped cream. They are different—and delicious!

BUTTER PECAN FLAN

¼ cup firmly packed light brown sugar
2 tablespoons butter
½ cup finely chopped pecans
6 eggs, slightly beaten
⅓ cup sugar
¼ teaspoon salt
2 cups milk, scalded
1 teaspoon vanilla
  maraschino cherries

To make hot water bath for the flan, place a 9-inch round cake pan in oven and pour water in pan until half full. Preheat oven to 350°F. Melt brown sugar and butter over low heat; stir in pecans. Press onto bottom of a 9-inch pie pan. Set aside. Mix eggs, sugar, and salt together until well blended. Slowly pour milk into egg mixture, stirring constantly. Add flavoring. Set lined pan in hot water bath in oven; pour in egg mixture. Bake until knife inserted halfway between center and outside edge comes out clean, 35 to 40 minutes. Remove promptly from hot water and refrigerate. Chill several hours. To serve, run a knife around edge of pie pan. Place serving plate on pie pan; invert. Shake to loosen. Garnish with maraschino cherries. Makes 6 servings.

CREAM CARAMEL FLAN

    ¾ cup sugar
    3 tablespoons water
    1 quart heavy cream
    ½ cup sugar
    1 teaspoon vanilla
    4 eggs
    4 egg yolks
       whipped cream, optional

Using a 10-inch metal pie plate, heat ¾ cup sugar and the water together until mixture caramelizes. Have a pan of cold water nearby; plunge the pie plate into the water to solidify the caramel, and quickly twirl it this way and that so the sides and bottom are completely coated with the caramel. Set the pie plate aside, to fill with the following cream: Scald cream, stir in sugar and vanilla; cool a little. Beat whole eggs and egg yolks together; when cream mixture has cooled a little, pour into eggs. Mix well. Pour into the prepared pie plate coated with caramel. Set it into another pan of water and bake at 350°F. for 35 to 40 minutes or until set, when an inserted knife will come out clean. Then cool and chill. To serve, invert the pie pan over a serving platter and remove the flan upside down so the caramel side is on top. Serve garnished with whipped cream, if desired.

RAISIN BREAD PUDDING

    8 slices raisin bread
    4 eggs, separated
    ¼ cup sugar
    3 cups milk
    1 teaspoon vanilla
    ½ teaspoon nutmeg
    1 10-ounce jar orange marmalade
    3 tablespoons sugar

Cut bread into ½-inch cubes. Place bread cubes in a shallow buttered 1½-quart baking dish. Beat egg yolks with ¼ cup sugar, milk, vanilla, and nutmeg. Pour over bread. Set baking dish in a pan containing 1 inch of hot water. Bake in a preheated 350°F. oven for 40 to 45 minutes or until center is firm to the touch. Remove dish from water and cool. Spread top of pudding with orange marmalade. Beat egg whites until foamy; beat in sugar, 1 tablespoon at a time, until mixture is stiff and glossy. Spoon meringue around outer edge of pudding. Bake in a preheated 350°F. oven 12 to 15 minutes or until meringue is lightly browned. Makes 6 servings.

PANTRY BREAD PUDDING

> 3 cups ½-inch cubes of firm-type white bread
> ½ cup coarsely chopped pitted prunes
> 4 eggs
> 2 cups milk
> 2 tablespoons sugar
> 1 teaspoon vanilla
> grated rind of small orange

Mix together bread cubes and chopped prunes; spoon mixture into 6 heavily buttered 6-ounce custard cups. Beat eggs with milk, sugar, vanilla, and orange rind. Pour mixture over bread cubes. Set custard cups in a pan containing 1 inch of hot water. Bake in a preheated 350°F. oven for 25 to 30 minutes or until centers are firm to the touch. Remove custard cups from water. Unmold each pudding and serve with warm Strawberry Sauce. Makes 6 servings.

> STRAWBERRY SAUCE:
> 1½ cups strawberry jam or preserves
> juice of 1 orange
> ¼ cup slivered toasted almonds

Combine jam, orange juice, and almonds. Cook over low heat, stirring, until jam melts.

PRUNE MERINGUE BREAD PUDDING

    1 cup pitted prunes
    8 slices day-old bread, cut in ½-inch cubes
    3 cups milk, scalded
    3 eggs, separated
    ¾ cup sugar
    2 tablespoons melted butter
    ¼ teaspoon salt
    1 teaspoon vanilla

Snip ½ cup of prunes; reserve remaining prunes for topping. Put bread cubes in a bowl and pour scalded milk over; let stand about 10 minutes. Beat egg yolks slightly and stir in. Add 6 tablespoons sugar, melted butter, salt, vanilla, and snipped prunes. Mix well. Pour into 1½-quart baking dish. Bake at 325°F. for 1 hour. Remove pudding from oven and cover with meringue made by beating egg whites stiff with remaining sugar.

FLAMING APPLE PUDDING

Decorate with rows of pitted prunes. Raise oven temperature to 400°F. Return pudding to oven and bake about 5 minutes longer, or until meringue is lightly golden. Makes 8 to 10 servings.

FLAMING APPLE PUDDING

> ½ cup butter
> 1 cup sugar
> 3 eggs
> 2 cups sifted flour
> 1 teaspoon baking powder
> ½ teaspoon baking soda
> 1 cup canned applesauce
> ⅓ cup mixed candied fruit
> ⅓ cup raisins
> ⅓ cup chopped nuts
> 1 teaspoon apple pie spice
> ¼ cup brandy

Cream butter until light and fluffy. Gradually add sugar and beat again until fluffy. Beat in eggs, one at a time. Fold in flour, baking powder, baking soda, and applesauce. Beat until smooth. Fold in fruit, raisins, nuts, and apple pie spice. Pour mixture into well-buttered and floured 1½ quart mold. Cover with greased foil and bake in a 300°F. oven for 1¼ hours. After 1 hour, remove foil and allow top to brown. Let pudding cool in pan for 5 minutes. Tap mold to loosen and invert on serving platter. Warm brandy and pour over pudding. Set aflame. Cut into wedges and serve hot with Apple Orange Sauce. Makes 6 to 8 servings.

> APPLE ORANGE SAUCE:
> 1 cup canned applesauce
> grated rind and juice of 1 small orange
> ⅓ cup sugar
> ⅓ cup flaked coconut
> 1 cup sour cream

Combine all ingredients and blend well. Chill until ready to serve. Makes about 2½ cups of sauce.

If you want to make a proper steamed pudding, do obtain a special mold for this purpose. It should have a tight fitting lid with a handle, and fluted sides to produce a prettily shaped pudding. Gourmet kitchen suppliers usually stock this item— well worth a few dollars for a once-in-a-lifetime purchase.

STEAMED CRANBERRY PUDDING

          6 tablespoons butter
          ¾ cup sugar
          2 eggs
         2¼ cups sifted flour
         2½ teaspoons baking powder
          ¼ teaspoon salt
          ½ cup milk
          2 cups cranberries
          ½ cup chopped pecans

In a large mixing bowl cream butter and sugar; add eggs, one at a time. Sift together flour, baking powder, and salt; add to creamed mixture alternately with milk. Stir in cranberries and pecans. Turn into a 6-cup buttered mold. If mold has its own lid, butter inside of lid and cover mold; or use foil to cover, pressing tightly around edges and securing with rubber band or string. Place mold on a rack in a pan with a tight-fitting cover. Pour enough water into pan to come halfway up on mold. Bring water to boil; cover and reduce heat to simmer. Steam 1½ to 2 hours until done. Let stand 10 minutes; unmold and serve with Eggnog Dessert Sauce. Pudding may be refrigerated several days or cooled, wrapped, and frozen for several months. To heat: thaw in refrigerator; wrap in foil and reheat at 325°F., about 45 minutes. Makes 10 to 12 servings.

          EGGNOG DESSERT SAUCE:
           1 cup butter
          1½ cups sugar
           1 cup dairy eggnog
           ½ teaspoon rum extract

In a saucepan combine butter, sugar, and eggnog; heat over low heat, stirring occasionally, until hot. Stir in extract. Makes 3 cups.

STEAMED CRANBERRY PUDDING

4

Luscious Trifles, Profiteroles, and Floating Islands

Custard and whipped cream abound in these desserts, but they include many other delicious ingredients as well. Clear deep bowls are a must for trifles, and crystal punch bowls are great for a crowd. Smaller clear bowls are best for profiteroles, and for both be sure to prolong the moment of viewing before you begin to spoon the dessert into individual plates. Half the fun of preparing these novelties is to enjoy the excitement they generate—so do leave them on the table as a conversation piece as you busy yourself with getting ready to serve. Remember, the beauty is in the presentation, so be sure to make the most of those moments.

Before you read the recipes, an explanation of origin and ingredients may be helpful:

A TRIFLE *is an English sweet pudding, made with pieces of cake smeared with jam and sometimes soaked with sherry or liqueur before being smothered in custard.*

PROFITEROLES *are tiny cream puffs filled with a custard and then smothered in whipped cream, or sometimes filled with the whipped cream and covered with a rich custard.*

FLOATING ISLANDS *are made with poached meringue balls either floating on top of—or smothered with—a rich custard sauce. They are served from a beautiful bowl much the same as trifles and profiteroles.*

In summer, this trifle often has a layer of fresh strawberries in its midst. You can add them and still be authentic.

TRADITIONAL ENGLISH TRIFLE

CUSTARD:

2 *cups milk*

3 *eggs, beaten*

2 *tablespoons sugar*

1 *teaspoon vanilla*

Pour ½ cup of the milk into the beaten eggs; add sugar and vanilla and beat until thickened. Scald remaining 1½ cups of milk; pour egg mixture into it and continue to cook and stir until mixture thickens. Do not bring to a boiling point as mixture may curdle. Cool.

TO ASSEMBLE THE TRIFLE:

12 *ladyfingers*

 raspberry jam

 8 *ounces sherry*

12 *macaroons*

 whipped cream

 almonds

 maraschino cherries

Split ladyfingers and spread generously with raspberry jam. Place half the ladyfingers in the bottom of a deep glass bowl; pour half the sherry over them. Arrange the rest of the ladyfingers and the macaroons on top of these, and pour the rest of the sherry over them. Pour the above custard over this, letting it trickle through. Chill. When ready to serve, top with whipped cream, almonds, and maraschino cherries, if desired. Makes 8 servings.

JELLY ROLL TRIFLE

> 2 recipes Jelly Roll (below)
> 1 cup sherry
> 1 recipe Custard (below)
> 1 pint heavy cream, whipped
>   slivered blanched almonds
>   maraschino cherries

Cut each jelly roll into 12 slices. Line bottom and sides of a large glass bowl with as many slices as needed. Pour ¾ cup of the sherry over slices in bowl; spread custard on top. Place remaining jelly roll slices over custard. Pour remaining ¼ cup sherry on cake; top with remaining custard. Chill 6 hours or overnight. Top Trifle with whipped cream. Garnish with slivered blanched almonds or cherries. Makes about 12 servings.

> JELLY ROLL:
> 1 teaspoon baking powder
> ¼ teaspoon salt
> 3 eggs
> ½ cup sugar
> ½ cup light corn syrup
> 1 cup sifted cake flour
> 1 teaspoon vanilla
> 1 cup raspberry preserves

Grease 15½- by 10½- by 1-inch baking pan; line bottom with waxed paper and grease again. Combine baking powder, salt, and eggs in mixing bowl with rotary beater or electric mixer. Beating constantly, add sugar gradually, then corn syrup 1 tablespoon at a time, beating until mixture is thick and light in color. Fold in flour and vanilla. Pour batter into prepared baking pan. Bake in 375°F. oven about 15 minutes or until cake springs back when lightly touched with finger. Immediately turn onto cloth sprinkled with confectioners' sugar. Remove waxed paper. Roll up in cloth, starting at narrow end; cool about 15 minutes. Unroll and spread with raspberry preserves, spreading almost to edges of cake. Roll up cake; wrap cloth around roll. Cool completely on wire rack. Makes 1 Jelly Roll.

CUSTARD:

½ *cup sugar*
5 *tablespoons cornstarch*
¼ *teaspoon salt*
4 *cups milk*
2 *eggs, well beaten*
1½ *teaspoons vanilla*

Mix together sugar, cornstarch, and salt in top of double boiler. Gradually stir in milk. Cook over boiling water, stirring constantly, until mixture is thickened. Cover; cook 10 minutes, stirring occasionally. Stir a small amount into beaten eggs, then stir into remaining hot mixture until well blended. Cook over boiling water 2 minutes, stirring constantly. Remove from heat; blend in vanilla. Cool slightly.

CUSTARD TRIFLE
(A Quick-trick Way)

1 *3-ounce package egg custard mix*
2½ *cups milk*
1 *8-inch sponge cake layer*
½ *cup raspberry jam*
1 *17-ounce can sliced peaches*
1 *cup heavy cream, whipped*
   maraschino cherries
   toasted slivered almonds

Prepare custard mix as directed on the package, increasing amount of milk to 2½ cups. Remove from heat; cool 30 minutes, stirring occasionally. Cover with wax paper; set aside. Split sponge cake into two layers. Spread jam on one layer; top with the other. Cut cake into small squares. Drain peaches, reserving ¾ cup syrup. Quickly dunk cake squares in the reserved syrup. Put half of the squares in a serving dish; cover with ½ cup sliced peaches. Top with half of the custard; continue layering, ending with custard. Garnish with whipped cream, cherries, and toasted slivered almonds. Makes 6 to 8 servings.

CONCORD GRAPE TRIFLE

> 4 egg yolks
> ½ cup sugar
> 2 teaspoons vanilla
> 1 cup milk
> 1 cup light cream
> 2 sponge cake layers, baked and cooled
> ½ cup sherry
> ½ cup Concord grape jam
> ⅓ cup shelled almonds
> 1 cup heavy cream
> 1 tablespoon sugar
> frosted grapes
> shelled almonds

In the top of a double boiler, beat egg yolks with ½ cup sugar until well blended. Add vanilla; stir in milk and light cream. Place over boiling water and cook, stirring constantly, until custard is thick enough to coat a wooden spoon, about 15 minutes. Chill several hours. Meanwhile, place a layer of sponge cake in a large crystal bowl. Pour ½ the sherry over the cake; spread with ½ cup Concord grape jam. Stud cake layer with ½ the almonds. Repeat with remaining layer. Refrigerate until ready to serve. Combine heavy cream and remaining 1 tablespoon sugar; beat until stiff. Just before serving, pour custard over cake layers. Top with whipped cream. Garnish with frosted grapes and additional almonds. Makes 8 to 10 servings.

CUSTARD TRIFLE

APPLE-RASPBERRY TRIFLE
(A Quick-trick Way)

      2 sponge cake layers, 8-inch size
      2 to 4 tablespoons sweet sherry
      1 3-ounce package instant vanilla pudding
     2½ cups milk
      ⅛ teaspoon almond extract
      1 20-ounce jar apple-raspberry sauce
      ½ cup heavy cream, whipped
      ¼ cup sliced, toasted almonds

Sprinkle each cake layer with 1 or 2 tablespoons sherry. Prepare instant pudding as package directs, using 2½ cups milk. Stir in almond extract. Place one cake layer in shallow glass serving dish. Top with half of pudding and half of apple-raspberry sauce. Cover with second cake layer. Top with remaining pudding and apple-raspberry sauce. Decorate with whipped cream and sliced almonds. Chill. Makes 8 servings.

ORANGE-SHERRY TRIFLE
(A Quick-trick Way)

      1 cooled baked 8-inch sponge cake layer
      ½ cup orange juice
      ¼ cup sherry wine
      2 tablespoons hot water
      ⅓ cup red raspberry preserves or orange marmalade
      ½ cup soft macaroon crumbs (optional)
      1 17½-ounce container frozen vanilla flavor pudding, thawed
      1 4½-ounce container frozen whipped topping
         almonds, whole or slivered, optional
         maraschino cherries, optional

Place cake layer on a plate. Combine orange juice and wine; sprinkle on both sides of cake to soak. Add hot water to preserves. Cut cake into 1½-inch cubes. Transfer to 1- or 1½-quart serving bowl or 8 individual

ORANGE-SHERRY TRIFLE

serving dishes. Drizzle preserve mixture over cake; then top with macaroon crumbs. Spoon pudding over crumbs. Chill at least 2 hours. Before
serving, top with whipped topping. Garnish with almonds and maraschino cherries, if desired. Makes 8 to 10 servings.

BLACK CHERRY TRIFLE
(A Quick-trick Way)

      1 baked 8-inch sponge layer, cooled
      1 3-ounce black cherry flavor gelatin
      1 cup boiling water
     ¾ cup cold water
     ½ cup sherry wine
     ¼ pound almond macaroons, crumbled
      1 3¾-ounce package vanilla instant pudding
    1½ cups cold milk
     ½ cup cold light cream
      1 16-ounce can pitted black cherries, well drained
      2 cups whipped cream
      3 tablespoons slivered almonds

Place sponge layer in a large bowl. Dissolve gelatin in boiling water. Add cold water and sherry. Pour over sponge layer. Chill until set, but not too firm. Remove layer and cut into squares; place into a large pretty glass bowl. Sprinkle with macaroon crumbs. Prepare pudding mix with milk and cream as directed on package. Do not overbeat; mixture will be thin. Add drained black cherries; pour at once over sponge squares. Chill until set—about 10 minutes—or until serving time. Garnish with whipped cream and slivered almonds. Makes 10 to 12 servings.

When in Rome, do as the Romans do—they serve large bowls of profiteroles. Here's one version that is superb.

MOCHA PROFITEROLES

      1 recipe Small Cream Puffs (page 196, Saint-Honoré Torte)
      1 recipe Cream Filling (page 197, Saint-Honoré Torte)
      2 cups heavy cream, whipped
      2 tablespoons cold strong coffee, preferably espresso
      1 teaspoon powdered instant coffee

Bake and fill the small cream puffs as directed. Pile them into a large glass bowl. Combine whipped cream with the mixture of strong coffee and powdered coffee. Fold whipped cream mixture carefully over the cream puffs so they are completely blanketed with the mixture. To serve, spoon several cream puffs and sauce onto individual serving plates. Makes 8 servings.

CHOCOLATE PROFITEROLES

> 1 recipe Small Cream Puffs (page 196, Saint-Honoré Torte)
> 1 cup heavy cream, whipped
> ¼ cup canned chocolate syrup
> 3 egg yolks
> ¼ cup sugar
> 1½ teaspoons cornstarch
> 2 cups milk
> ¼ cup canned chocolate syrup
> 3 egg whites

Bake and fill the small cream puffs with a mixture of whipped cream and ¼ cup chocolate syrup, being careful to fold the syrup through the whipped cream without breaking down the air bubbles. Pile the filled puffs into a large glass bowl. In a saucepan, stir together egg yolks, sugar, and cornstarch. Stir in milk and chocolate syrup. Heat and stir constantly until mixture thickens. Remove from heat and cool. Beat egg whites until stiff. Combine the cooled chocolate mixture with the egg whites by folding them together with care. Pour mixture over the cream puffs until they are completely blanketed with it. To serve, spoon several cream puffs and sauce onto individual serving plates. Makes 8 servings.

PROFITEROLES IN CUSTARD SAUCE

> 1 recipe Small Cream Puffs (page 196, Saint-Honoré Torte)
> 1 recipe Cream Filling (page 197, Saint-Honoré Torte)
> 2 cups heavy cream
> 2 tablespoons confectioners' sugar

Bake small cream puffs. Prepare recipe for cream filling. Whip heavy cream, gradually adding confectioners' sugar. Fill cream puffs with some of the whipped cream mixture. Pile them into a large glass bowl. Pour prepared Cream Filling over the cream puffs, prodding here and there with a spatula so sauce can seep all the way down. Use remaining whipped cream as garnish around the top of the bowl. Makes 8 servings.

Floating Islands is an old-fashioned dessert that has never lost its charm. This is the traditional way of serving it—and following are two variations. In one version you will find the poached meringues covered with custard sauce, much as profiteroles are in le grand cuisine of Europe. The other is served individually with a base layer of fruit covered with custard and topped with one poached meringue per serving. Whichever you choose to serve will produce gasps of gustatory pleasure.

FLOATING ISLANDS

> ½ recipe for Snow Eggs (page 61), using 2 cups milk
> 4 egg yolks
> ¼ cup sugar
> 1½ teaspoons cornstarch
> 1 teaspoon vanilla

Measure the milk used for poaching and add enough milk to equal 2 cups; pour into a saucepan. Beat egg yolks, sugar, and cornstarch together, until thick. Stir into warm milk in saucepan. Stir in vanilla. Heat and stir constantly, until mixture gets very thick, about 4 minutes. Pour into a shallow compote bowl and cover with plastic wrap to prevent skin from forming over the top. Chill. Chill Snow Eggs separately too. Then just before serving, remove the plastic wrap and carefully place the Snow Eggs over the top of the custard. Makes 4 to 6 servings.

EGGS À LA NEIGE

> 2 egg whites
> ¼ teaspoon cream of tartar
> ½ cup sugar
> water
> 1 tablespoon cornstarch
> ¼ teaspoon salt
> 2 egg yolks
> 2 cups light cream or milk
> 1 teaspoon vanilla
> fruit *
> unsweetened chocolate, flaked

Beat egg whites and cream of tartar until foamy. Add ¼ cup sugar. Beat until stiff peaks form when beater is raised. Half fill deep skillet with water. Bring water almost to boil; turn off heat. Drop egg white mixture by mounds into water. Cover 1 minute. Drain on absorbent paper. Chill meringues 1 to 2 hours. Combine remaining ¼ cup sugar, cornstarch, and salt in double boiler top. Mix in egg yolks, then cream or milk. Cook over boiling water, stirring constantly, until mixture is slightly thickened, about 5 minutes. Remove from boiling water; cool. Stir in vanilla. Chill. Arrange fruit in bottom of deep dish. Put meringues on top. Gently pour custard sauce over all. Sprinkle with flaked chocolate. Makes 4 to 6 servings.

* Use *one* of the following:
1 pint strawberries, hulled and sliced
or
2 eating oranges, sectioned, and 2 bananas, sliced
or
1 12-ounce can mandarin orange sections, drained, and
1 pound grapes, seeded

Before starting this recipe, be sure you have 14 eggs on hand. (The extra egg yolks may be saved for future use by covering with water and refrigerating for a day or two.) The recipe has many steps, but the results will be mouthfuls of fabulous fluff.

SNOW EGGS IN COFFEE CUSTARD SAUCE

SNOW EGGS:

8 egg whites
1 cup sugar
1 quart milk

Beat 8 egg whites until frothy; then continue beating and gradually add 1 cup of sugar. Beat until egg whites are stiff enough to stand in very firm peaks. Pour milk into a large skillet; heat just to a simmer, keeping the heat very low thereafter. With a tablespoon in one hand to scoop up a heaping portion of the egg whites, and the back of another spoon or spatula in the other hand to round the shape of the top, carefully make oval balls (like eggs) of the mixture, and slide each "egg" into the simmering milk. Let them poach for 2 minutes, not touching each other, and then gently turn each over to poach on the other side for a minute longer. Lift each snow egg out of the simmering milk with a slotted spoon and place it on a flat pan, lined with paper toweling, to drain. Continue the procedure until all the beaten egg white is poached. Then measure the remaining milk, adding more if necessary to increase again to 1 quart, and pour into a large saucepan.

COFFEE CUSTARD SAUCE:

6 egg yolks
½ cup sugar
1 tablespoon cornstarch
1 teaspoon vanilla
1 tablespoon instant coffee
6 egg whites

EGGS À LA NEIGE

Beat 6 egg yolks, add sugar, cornstarch, and vanilla; stir into reserved milk. Cook over low heat, stirring until mixture thickens. Stir in instant coffee until completely dissolved. Remove from heat and cool, while you beat the remaining 6 egg whites until stiff. Then combine the two mixtures by folding them gently together. Using a large glass bowl, as for trifle recipes, place several of the snow eggs in the bottom of the bowl; pour some custard sauce over them, and repeat until the entire quantity of poached snow eggs is covered with custard sauce. Chill for several hours until serving time, covering top of bowl with plastic wrap to prevent skin from forming. Spoon out on individual serving plates at the table. Makes 8 to 12 servings.

5

Shimmering Gelatin Molds

Gelatin is a wonderful ingredient to use when you want a mixture that will hold its shape after a mold is removed. The prettier the mold, the more enticing your dessert will be.

If you are trying to avoid the use of whipped cream or beaten eggs, this is the chapter for you, for these desserts combine light-caloried ingredients in most instances and still manage to create the illusion of forbidden sweets.

The rules to remember when working with gelatin are few: dissolve the granules completely, mix well, do not add extra liquid, and be sure to chill for enough hours to make a firm dessert.

When unmolding, dip a towel in hot water, wring out, and wrap around the mold. Or if you prefer, dip the mold quickly up to its rim in warm water and then invert on a platter. If, despite these two excellent methods, you seem to have bad luck when removing molds, try lightly coating the mold beforehand with a high-grade, tasteless salad oil. Or place strips of aluminum foil into the molds first, leaving ends overlapping the edges—then pull on the strips to release the bond of the gelatin to the mold, invert, and slip the contents out.

Do present the shimmering molded dessert on a lovely platter or footed cake stand for an effective display. It gives it a company manner.

SPICED COFFEE JELLY

SPICED COFFEE JELLY

>   2 *envelopes (2 tablespoons) unflavored gelatin*
> 3½ *cups cold strong coffee*
>   2 *sticks cinnamon*
>   6 *whole cloves*
> ⅔ *cup sugar*
> ⅛ *teaspoon salt*

Soften gelatin in ½ cup cold coffee in small cup. In saucepan combine remaining 3 cups of coffee, stick of cinnamon, and whole cloves. Bring to a boil; reduce heat and simmer 5 minutes. Remove cinnamon and cloves. Add softened gelatin and stir until dissolved. Stir in sugar and salt. Pour into 4-cup mold; chill until firm. Unmold and serve with whipped topping. Makes 8 servings.

Note: If desired, instant coffee may be used. Use 3½ cups of cold water and 4 tablespoons of regular instant coffee powder.

CREAMY ORANGE-PINEAPPLE MOLD

>   2 *envelopes (2 tablespoons) unflavored gelatin*
> ½ *cup cold water*
>   1 *20½-ounce can crushed pineapple, undrained*
> ⅔ *cup orange juice*
> ⅓ *cup lemon juice*
> ⅓ *cup sugar*
>   2 *cups dairy sour cream*
>   2 *cups sliced strawberries*
> ½ *cup chopped pecans*

In a 1½-quart saucepan sprinkle gelatin over water to soften. Heat over low heat, stirring constantly, until gelatin is dissolved. Stir in pineapple, with syrup, orange and lemon juices and sugar; stir until sugar is dissolved. Pour into a large bowl; chill until jelly-like in consistency. Stir sour cream into gelatin mixture; fold in strawberries and nuts. Turn into a 7-cup mold; chill until set. Makes 8 to 10 servings.

BROKEN WINDOW-GLASS CAKE
(A Quick-trick Way)

> 1 3-ounce package orange flavor gelatin
> 1 3-ounce package cherry flavor gelatin
> 1 3-ounce package lime flavor gelatin
> 3 cups boiling water
> 1½ cups cold water
> 1 3-ounce package lemon flavor gelatin
> ¼ cup sugar
> 1 cup boiling water
> ½ cup canned pineapple juice
> 1½ cups graham cracker crumbs
> ⅓ cup butter, melted
> 2 cups heavy cream, whipped, or 4 cups (one 9-ounce
> container) frozen whipped topping, thawed

Prepare the orange, cherry, and lime gelatins separately, dissolving each in 1 cup boiling water; then add ½ cup cold water to each. Pour each flavor into a separate 8-inch square pan. Chill until firm—at least 4 hours or overnight. Dissolve lemon gelatin and sugar in 1 cup boiling water; stir in pineapple juice. Chill until slightly thickened. Meanwhile, mix graham cracker crumbs with melted butter. If desired, set aside about ¼ cup for a garnish. Press crumb mixture smoothly over bottom and sides to within 1 inch from top of a 9-inch spring form pan. Blend whipped topping into the slightly thickened lemon gelatin. Cut the firm gelatin in the three pans into ½-inch cubes; fold into the whipped topping mixture. Spoon into crumb-lined spring form pan. Chill until firm—at least 7 hours or overnight. Just before serving, run a spatula around sides of pan; then gently remove sides. Garnish top with the remaining ¼ cup crumbs. Makes 16 servings.

You get a great head start, with no excuses needed, when you use frozen lemonade concentrate in this dessert. One of the conveniences of living in the twentieth century!

LEMONEGG FLUFF

  3 *envelopes (3 tablespoons) unflavored gelatin*
½ *cup sugar*
    dash of salt
  1 *cup water*
10 *egg yolks, beaten*
  1 *6-ounce can frozen lemonade concentrate, undiluted*
10 *egg whites*
½ *cup sugar*

Combine gelatin, sugar, and salt in a heavy saucepan; add water. Cook over medium low heat, stirring constantly, until gelatin is dissolved. Add a small amount of the gelatin mixture to egg yolks and blend. Return egg yolk mixture to saucepan and continue cooking, stirring constantly, 2 minutes longer. Do not let mixture boil. Remove from heat. Stir in lemonade concentrate. Chill mixture until partially set (a syrupy consistency). Meanwhile, beat egg whites until frothy. Gradually add sugar and continue beating until stiff peaks form. Fold into gelatin mixture. Pour into a 2-quart mold and chill until firm. Unmold and serve with Cherry-Cinnamon Sauce. Makes 12 servings.

    CHERRY-CINNAMON SAUCE:
  1 *1-pound can tart red cherries*
½ *cup sugar*
  3 *tablespoons cinnamon red-hot candies*
  2 *tablespoons cornstarch*
  1 *tablespoon lemon juice*

Drain cherries, reserving juice. Combine sugar, cinnamon candies, and cornstarch in a saucepan. Add cherry juice and cook over medium heat, stirring constantly, until mixture thickens and is clear. Remove from heat. Add lemon juice and cherries. Cool before serving. Makes 2¼ cups.

ORANGE-CHEDDAR CHEESE MOLD

> ¾ cup orange juice
> 1 3-ounce package orange flavor gelatin
> 1 cup cottage cheese
> 1 cup dairy sour cream
> ¾ cup finely chopped celery
> ½ cup shredded Cheddar cheese
> 2 tablespoons lemon juice
>   fresh fruit for garnish

Heat orange juice to boiling point; pour over gelatin in small mixing bowl and stir until dissolved. Chill until consistency of unbeaten egg white. Beat gelatin mixture about 5 minutes. Fold in cottage cheese, sour cream, celery, Cheddar cheese, and lemon juice; turn into 5-cup salad mold. Chill until firm. Unmold and serve garnished with fresh fruit. Makes 6 servings.

LIME CHIFFON MOLD

> ¼ cup finely chopped or ground walnuts
> ¼ cup graham cracker crumbs
> 2 teaspoons sugar
> 1 tablespoon butter, melted
> 1 3-ounce package lime flavor gelatin
> ½ cup sugar
> 1 cup boiling water
> ½ cup cold water
> 2 tablespoons lime juice
> 2 teaspoons grated lime rind
> 3 drops green food coloring (optional)
> 2 cups (one 4½-ounce container) frozen whipped topping,
>   thawed
>   grated or slivered lime rind or lime slices, optional

Combine nuts, crumbs, and 2 teaspoons sugar; add butter and blend well. Press mixture evenly onto bottom and sides of buttered 1-quart mold.

Chill about 20 minutes. Meanwhile, dissolve gelatin and ½ cup sugar in boiling water; add cold water, lime juice, lime rind, and food coloring. Chill until slightly thickened. Set aside ¼ cup whipped topping for garnish. Blend remaining whipped topping into gelatin mixture with wire whip or rotary beater until smooth. Chill again until slightly thickened. Pour into crumb-lined mold. Chill 3 or 4 hours or until set. Dip mold carefully into warm water, loosen sides with spatula, and turn out onto serving plate. Garnish with reserved whipped topping and lime rind or slices. Serves 6 to 8.

COCONUT RICE IMPERIAL

    1½ cups milk
    ⅔ cup packaged enriched precooked rice
    ¾ teaspoon salt
     1 envelope (1 tablespoon) unflavored gelatin
     2 tablespoons cold water
     2 egg yolks
    ½ cup sugar
    ½ teaspoon orange extract
    1¼ teaspoons grated orange rind
    1⅓ cups flaked coconut
     1 cup heavy cream
        fruit, optional

Scald milk in saucepan. Add rice and salt. Mix just to moisten all rice. Cover; remove from heat. Let stand about 5 minutes, fluffing occasionally with a fork. Meanwhile, soften gelatin in cold water. Combine egg yolks and sugar. Add a few spoonfuls of the hot rice mixture to egg yolks and sugar. Mix well. Then add egg yolk mixture to hot rice in saucepan. Add the softened gelatin, orange extract, grated orange rind, and coconut. Mix well. Chill until mixture begins to thicken. Whip cream just until soft peaks form; fold into thickened rice mixture. Pour into 1-quart mold. Chill until firm. Unmold. Serve with raspberries, strawberries, or other fruit, if desired. Makes 4 cups or 8 servings.

ORANGE RICE IMPERIAL

> 1 cup uncooked regular rice
> 3½ cups milk
> 2 tablespoons butter
> ½ teaspoon salt
> 1 envelope (1 tablespoon) unflavored gelatin
> 1 cup orange juice, divided
> 2 eggs, separated
> ¾ cup sugar, divided
> 2 tablespoons grated orange rind
> ½ cup chopped marrons (from drained chestnuts in brandy
>   syrup), optional
> 1 cup heavy cream, whipped
> 4 oranges, sectioned
> ⅓ cup sliced marrons, optional

Combine rice, milk, butter, and salt in large heavy saucepan. Bring to a boil; reduce heat. Stir with a fork, cover, and simmer 30 to 40 minutes, or until rice is tender and most of liquid is absorbed. Sprinkle gelatin over ½ cup orange juice; let stand until gelatin is moistened. Beat egg yolks with remaining ½ cup orange juice. Add softened gelatin, egg yolk mixture, and ½ cup sugar to cooked rice; mix well. Stir over low heat for 2 or 3 minutes, until slightly thickened. Remove from heat; stir in grated orange rind and chopped chestnuts. Chill, stirring occasionally, until mixture is completely cooled and mounds slightly when dropped from a spoon. Beat egg whites until stiff but not dry; gradually add remaining ¼ cup sugar and beat until very stiff. Fold into rice mixture. Fold in whipped cream. Turn into 8-cup mold. Chill until set, several hours or overnight. Unmold and serve with orange sections mixed with sliced chestnuts. Makes 12 servings.

ORANGE RICE IMPERIAL

CHERRY COTTAGE DESSERT

> 1 30-ounce can pitted dark sweet cherries in heavy syrup
> 1 13½-ounce can crushed pineapple
> 2 envelopes (2 tablespoons) unflavored gelatin
> ½ cup pineapple syrup
> 2 cups cottage cheese
> ½ cup dairy sour cream
> ½ cup chopped pecans
> 1 tablespoon sugar
> 1 teaspoon grated lemon rind (optional)
> 1 tablespoon lemon juice
> ⅛ teaspoon salt
> ½ cup heavy cream, whipped

Drain cherries, reserving 1 cup syrup for sauce. Halve cherries; set aside ½ cup for sauce. Drain pineapple, reserving ½ cup syrup for gelatin mixture and 1 tablespoon for sauce; set aside. In a 1-quart saucepan soften gelatin in ½ cup pineapple syrup. Place over low heat, stirring constantly, until gelatin is dissolved. Cool slightly. In a bowl combine cottage cheese, sour cream, pecans, sugar, lemon rind and juice, salt, cherries, pineapple, and dissolved gelatin. Fold in whipped cream. Turn into a 7-cup mold; chill until set. Serve with Cherry Sauce. Makes 10 to 12 servings.

CHERRY SAUCE:

> ¼ cup sugar
> 2 tablespoons cornstarch
>   dash of salt
> 1 cup cherry syrup
> 1 teaspoon grated lemon rind
> 2 tablespoons lemon juice
> 1 tablespoon pineapple syrup
> ½ cup dark sweet cherries

In a 1-quart saucepan combine sugar, cornstarch, and salt. Stir in cherry syrup. Cook over medium heat, stirring constantly, until thickened. Cook 2 additional minutes. Stir in lemon rind and juice and pineapple syrup. Add cherries. Chill sauce. Spoon over dessert and serve. Makes about 2 cups of sauce.

RICE CREAM WITH RHUBARB TOPPING

> 1 envelope (1 tablespoon) unflavored gelatin
> 1½ cups milk
> 1 3-ounce package cream cheese, softened
> 2 eggs, separated
> ¼ cup sugar
> 1 cup cooked rice
> 1 teaspoon vanilla

Soften gelatin in ½ cup milk. Blend remaining milk with cream cheese. Stir in lightly beaten egg yolks and half of sugar. Add gelatin. Cook over low heat, stirring constantly, until mixture coats the spoon. Add rice and vanilla; cool slightly. Beat egg whites until frothy, then gradually beat in sugar, continuing beating until whites are stiff. Gently fold into rice mixture. Turn into a 1-quart mold. Chill until firm. Cut into wedges and serve with Rhubarb Topping. Serves 6 to 8.

> RHUBARB TOPPING:
> ½ pound pink rhubarb
> ¼ cup sugar
> ⅛ teaspoon salt
> ¼ cup light corn syrup
> 2 teaspoons cornstarch
> 2 tablespoons cold water

Wash rhubarb, discard ends of stalks and leaves, and cut stalks into 1-inch lengths. Mix sugar with salt and light corn syrup; add rhubarb and heat to boiling, then simmer 10 minutes or until rhubarb is tender. Mix cornstarch with cold water and stir into sauce; continue cooking, stirring, until sauce thickens and clears. Serve warm or cold.

6

Embellished Ice Creams and Sherbets

One of the discoveries Marco Polo brought back from his trip to the Far East was the fruit-flavored ices that became the forerunner of Italian sherbets and ice creams. Other countries of Europe were soon making these chilled treats in many flavors and textures, until today ice cream is probably the most popular dessert in the world.

The same substance that is quickly scooped on top of a child's cone, and then skillfully licked to the last sweet drop, can become the basis of an elegant dessert. Add some fruit or sauce, fill a mold with multicolored layers, encase it in meringue, or roll it up in cake—you'll find dozens of intriguing ideas in this chapter to tantalize your taste buds.

The success of your ice-cream or sherbet dessert will depend upon the quality you purchase. Do try to find a fine-textured, high-butterfat content ice cream for best results. It may be among the most expensive ice creams, but it will be able to stand up to the softening and refreezing that is called for in some of the recipes.

Included also are several do-it-yourself sherbet creations, with a few that are dietetic deceptions. All of these can be prepared in advance and held in your freezer until serving time.

STRAWBERRY ICE-CREAM BOMBE

> 2 pints strawberry ice cream
> 2 egg yolks
> ⅓ cup sugar
> 1 tablespoon lemon rind
> 2 tablespoons lemon juice
> 1 tablespoon cold water
> 1 egg white
> 2 tablespoons sugar
> 1 cup heavy cream, whipped
>   fresh strawberries, optional

Chill a 7-cup mold in freezer. Quickly spread ice cream as evenly as possible with back of spoon or spatula on inside of mold to make a shell lining about ½-inch thick. Return to freezer to harden. Meanwhile, in top of double boiler beat egg yolks well. Beat in ⅓ cup sugar, lemon rind and juice, and water. Cook, stirring constantly, over rapidly boiling water until thickened (about 10 minutes). Cool completely. In a small mixing bowl beat egg white until frothy. Gradually beat in 2 tablespoons sugar; beat until stiff peaks form. Fold in lemon mixture; then whipped cream. Pour into ice-cream-lined mold. Freeze. To unmold: Dip into warm water and turn out onto chilled plate. Garnish with fresh strawberries, if desired. Serves 6 to 8.

APRICOT ICE-CREAM MOLD

> ½ cup apricot preserves
> ½ cup sliced toasted almonds
> 2 pints coffee ice cream, softened

Chill 4-cup mold in freezer. In a small bowl combine preserves and almonds. Press into bottom and part way up the sides of mold. Freeze until firm. Press ice cream into mold. Return to freezer to harden. To unmold, dip into warm water and turn out onto chilled plate. Return to freezer to harden. Makes 6 servings.

SPUMONI MOLD

This recipe gives you a choice of vanilla or chocolate ice cream for the outside layer of the Spumoni. Use chocolate for greater contrast in color and taste—or make a thin layer of each. Whichever you choose, this Italian favorite will be a hit.

SPUMONI MOLD

> 1 *quart chocolate or vanilla ice cream*
> ½ *cup cold milk*
> 1 *tablespoon instant coffee*
> 1 *envelope whipped topping mix*
> ½ *cup maraschino cherries, quartered*
> ¼ *cup toasted, slivered, blanched almonds*

Line 8- by 4-inch loaf pan or 2-quart mixing bowl with aluminum foil. Soften ice cream in a bowl. Press softened ice cream firmly onto sides and bottom of loaf pan or mixing bowl, leaving a hollow in the center. Freeze. Meanwhile, blend milk, instant coffee, and whipped topping mix in a deep, narrow-bottomed bowl. Beat with rotary beater or electric mixer at high speed until topping peaks. Continue beating until topping is light, fluffy, and fully whipped—about 2 minutes longer. Fold in cherries and toasted almonds. Spoon whipped topping mixture into center of ice-cream shell. Cover with aluminum foil and freeze at least 8 hours or overnight. Before serving, remove aluminum foil covering and unmold. Remove aluminum foil lining from dessert. If desired, garnish with prepared whipped topping, maraschino cherry halves, and toasted whole almonds. Makes 8 to 10 servings.

PRUNE ICE-CREAM BOMBE WITH
FLAMING PRUNE JUBILEE

> ½ cup pitted prunes
> ½ cup orange liqueur
> 1 quart vanilla ice cream
> 1 cup heavy cream, whipped

Sliver prunes and soak in orange liqueur overnight. Using a whisk or
heavy fork, beat ice cream until slightly softened. Fold slivered prunes
into ice cream. Then fold whipped cream into mixture, blending well.
Turn into chilled 6-cup mold and freeze until firm. When ready to serve,
dip mold briefly in deep pan of hot water to loosen and invert onto a silver
tray. Serve with Flaming Prune Jubilee Sauce. Makes 6 to 8 servings.

> FLAMING PRUNE JUBILEE SAUCE:
> ½ cup brandy-soaked prunes
> 1 cup orange juice
>   grated rind of 1 orange
> ½ cup sugar
> ½ cup orange liqueur (Grand Marnier, or other)

Remove prunes from brandy and sliver. Stir orange juice, rind, and sugar
together over low heat until sugar is melted. Add prunes and their juice
and simmer 2 minutes. Stir in liqueur. Ignite with match, and spoon,
flaming, over ice-cream bombe.

MINCEMEAT ICE-CREAM BOMBE

> 1 *quart orange sherbet*
> 1 *quart vanilla ice cream*
> 1 *8-inch cake layer*
> 1 *cup heavy cream, whipped*
>   *Mincemeat Sauce*

Chill a 6- to 8-cup mold in freezer at least 1 hour. With back of a spoon, press sherbet around inside of mold to make a shell. Freeze 1 hour or until firm. Fill center with vanilla ice cream, pressing firmly. Cover. Freeze 3 hours or until firm.

To unmold: Place cake layer on sheet of foil. Wipe outside of mold with hot damp cloth. Invert mold on cake. Gently shake mold to remove ice cream. Wrap and place in freezer until serving time. Before serving, decorate with whipped cream. Let stand 5 minutes for easier serving. Serve with Mincemeat Sauce. Makes 12 servings.

MINCEMEAT SAUCE:
> 1 *9-ounce package condensed mincemeat*
> ½ *cup light corn syrup*
> ½ *cup water*
> 2 *tablespoons rum*

Break mincemeat into small pieces in medium saucepan. Add light corn syrup, water, and rum. Stirring to break up pieces, bring to a boil over low heat and boil 1 minute. Serve warm or cool on ice cream. Makes 2 cups.

PEACH ICE-CREAM MERINGUE

½ cup butter
1¼ cups sugar
4 eggs, separated
⅔ cup cake flour
1 teaspoon baking powder
¼ teaspoon salt
¼ cup milk
¼ teaspoon cream of tartar
1 teaspoon vanilla
⅓ cup sliced almonds
1 pint peach ice cream

Butter 2 round 9-inch cake pans; line with waxed paper; set aside. In a mixing bowl cream butter; gradually add ½ cup sugar and beat until light and fluffy. Add egg yolks and beat well. Sift together flour, baking powder, and salt. Add to creamed mixture alternately with milk, beginning and ending with dry ingredients. Pour into pans. In a small mixing bowl sprinkle cream of tartar over egg whites. Beat until stiff. Add vanilla. Gradually beat in remaining ¾ cup sugar, beating constantly until dissolved. Divide onto top of cake batter. Sprinkle nuts over meringue in one pan. Bake in preheated 350°F. oven 30 to 40 minutes. Cool in pans 5 minutes. Turn out of pans onto wire racks. Place cake side down on racks. To serve: Place layer without nuts on serving plate, cake side down. Slice ice cream over layer. Top with remaining cake layer, meringue side up. Makes 10 to 12 servings.

PEACH ICE-CREAM MERINGUE—ON LEFT

STRAWBERRY ICE-CREAM BOMBE—ON RIGHT

Baked Alaska has a base of sponge cake, covered with ice cream and meringue. It is easy to prepare and fun to serve—if you follow a few simple rules. Start with very hard ice cream. (If you have softened it to shape it, return it to the freezer to harden before placing it in the oven.) Seal the meringue to the edges of the cake and bake at high heat for a few minutes. This will brown the top without melting the ice cream below. Serve at once, and return leftovers to the freezer if you want a dripless tablecloth!

BAKED ALASKA

    sponge, angel food, or pound loaf cake
8 *egg whites*
¼ *teaspoon cream of tartar*
¼ *teaspoon salt*
1 *cup sugar*
1 *teaspoon vanilla*
½ *gallon ice cream (your favorite flavor)*

Cut enough ½-inch slices of cake to make a rectangle, 8 by 6 inches. Cover two thicknesses of corrugated cardboard, 9 by 7 inches, with aluminum foil. Place cake on foil. Freeze. Let egg whites stand at room temperature for 1 hour. Beat egg whites until frothy. Add cream of tartar and salt; continue beating until soft peaks form when beater is slowly raised. Gradually beat in sugar, 2 tablespoons at a time, beating well after each addition. Continue beating for 5 minutes. Add vanilla. Place ice cream on cake base. (Start with very hard ice cream; if you have softened it to shape it, return it to the freezer to harden before placing it in the oven.) Working quickly, spread ice cream and cake with meringue, spreading down onto the foil, sealing the meringue completely to the edges of the cake. Make swirls on top and sides. Return to freezer until ready to serve—2 hours or more. Twenty minutes before serving, preheat oven to 425°F. Place the Alaska on cookie sheet. Bake 7 to 8 minutes on lowest shelf in oven. This baking at high heat will brown the top without melting the ice cream below. Remove to chilled platter. Serve at once. Makes 12 to 16 servings.

Note: Alaska can be prepared 1 or 2 days ahead and stored unwrapped in freezer. Bake as above.

PRUNE ALASKA

> 1½ cups pitted prunes
> ½ cup brandy, rum, sherry, or orange juice
> 1 8-inch sponge layer cake
> 3 egg whites
> ¼ teaspoon salt
> ½ teaspoon vanilla
> ½ cup granulated sugar
> 1 pint coffee or vanilla ice cream

Halve prunes, place in small pan and add brandy, rum, sherry, or orange juice. Cover. Bring to a boil; then remove from heat. Allow to stand, covered, for 2 hours or overnight. Line a cookie sheet with plain brown paper and place cake layer in center. Spoon prunes and liquid over cake to cover surface completely. Beat egg whites with salt and vanilla until frothy. Add sugar gradually and beat until peaks are stiff but not dry. Cut hard-frozen ice cream into 1-inch slices and arrange over prunes. Completely cover surface and sides of cake with meringue. Bake in a hot 425°F. oven 4 to 5 minutes, until peaks are a delicate golden brown. Slide onto a chilled platter and serve immediately. Makes 6 to 8 servings.

BRANDIED PRUNE ICE-CREAM CAKE

 1 *12-ounce package pitted prunes*
 1 *cup brandy*
 ½ *cup mixed candied peel*
 2 *8-inch sponge layers (store bought, mix, or homemade)*
 ½ *pint chocolate ice cream*
 ½ *pint pistachio ice cream*
 ½ *pint strawberry ice cream*
 ½ *pint vanilla ice cream*
 1 *cup heavy cream*
 ¼ *cup confectioners' sugar*
 ½ *teaspoon vanilla*

Snip prunes in small pieces. Place in saucepan with brandy. Cover. Bring to boil; then remove from heat and stir in candied peel. Cover and let stand until liquid is absorbed (about 1 to 2 hours). Stir occasionally. Cut sponge layers in half to make four layers. Soften ice cream slightly before spreading. Place 1 sponge layer in 8-inch spring form pan. Spread to edges first with chocolate ice cream, then ¾ cup prune mixture. Add second layer, pistachio ice cream and ¾ cup prune mixture. Place in freezer for 30 minutes; then add third sponge layer, strawberry ice cream, remaining prune mixture, and fourth sponge layer. Top with vanilla ice cream. Arrange bits of prune into a star-shaped design in center. Place cake in freezer for 30 minutes longer. Whip cream with confectioners' sugar and vanilla until firm. Remove cake from freezer and allow to stand 1 minute before unmolding. Spread whipped cream on sides of cake and reserve some to pipe around edges with a pastry tube, or spoon mounds of whipped cream around edge, to garnish. Return cake to freezer until serving time. Makes 12 to 16 servings.

PINEAPPLE-CHERRY-ALMOND PIE

CRUST:

1 cup sifted flour
¼ teaspoon salt
5 tablespoons butter
3 tablespoons milk

In a large bowl sift together flour and salt. Cut in butter until mixture resembles small peas. Sprinkle milk over flour mixture, 1 tablespoon at a time, mixing lightly with fork after each addition. Gather up dough with fingers; shake into a ball. On lightly floured board flatten ball of dough slightly and roll ⅛ inch thick into a circle 1 inch longer than diameter of 9-inch pie plate. Fold circle in half over rolling pin. Lift onto pie plate and ease pastry into pie plate. Fold extra dough over and build up on rim of pie plate. Flute edge. Prick bottom and side well with a fork. Bake in a preheated 450°F. oven about 10 minutes or until lightly browned. Cool, then place pie crust in freezer while preparing filling. Makes 6 to 8 servings.

FILLING:

3 pints vanilla ice cream
½ cup almond macaroon crumbs
½ cup toasted, sliced, blanched almonds
½ cup drained and chopped maraschino cherries
¼ cup well-drained crushed pineapple
½ cup heavy cream, whipped
1 teaspoon almond extract
2 drops red food coloring
   sweetened whipped cream
   quartered maraschino cherries

In a mixing bowl beat ice cream only until smooth but still thick. (Do not overbeat.) Fold in crumbs, almonds, cherries, pineapple, whipped cream, almond extract, and red food coloring. Mound mixture into chilled shell; freeze several hours or overnight. Garnish with additional whipped cream and maraschino cherries, if desired.

BAKED ALASKA PIE

CRUST:

1 cup flour
3 tablespoons confectioners' sugar
½ cup butter, softened
⅓ cup finely chopped nuts

In a small mixing bowl beat together flour, sugar, and butter until well blended. Stir in nuts. Press on bottom and sides of a 9-inch pie plate, building up edge; prick with fork. In a preheated 350°F. oven bake for 15 to 18 minutes or until lightly browned. Cool on wire rack: chill.

FILLING:

2 pints cherry ice cream, softened
1 pint vanilla ice cream, softened

Spoon 1 pint cherry ice cream into crust; pack down with back of spoon. Freeze. Repeat with vanilla ice cream and remaining 1 pint cherry ice cream. Cover and store in freezer. Just before serving prepare meringue.

MERINGUE:

2 egg whites
⅛ teaspoon cream of tartar
¼ cup sugar

In a small mixing bowl beat egg whites until frothy. Add cream of tartar and beat until soft peaks form. Add sugar, 1 tablespoon at a time, and beat until stiff peaks form. Spread meringue over ice cream, making certain it is sealed to crust. Place pie plate on wooden board. Bake in a preheated 500°F. oven for 1 to 3 minutes or until meringue is lightly browned. Serve immediately. Makes 6 to 8 servings.

BAKED ALASKA PIE

STRAWBERRY-PINEAPPLE PIE

STRAWBERRY-PINEAPPLE PIE

CRUST:

   1⅓ cups graham cracker crumbs
   ½ teaspoon cinnamon
   ¼ cup butter, melted

In a small bowl mix together crumbs and cinnamon; stir in butter. Reserve 2 tablespoons crumb mixture. Press remaining crumbs firmly and evenly against bottom and sides of 9-inch pie plate. Bake in preheated 350°F. oven for 5 minutes. Cool.

FILLING:

2 *pints strawberry ice cream, softened*
1 *20½-ounce can crushed pineapple, well drained*
  strawberries for garnish

In a large mixing bowl beat ice cream until smooth; beat in pineapple. Turn into crumb crust. Sprinkle reserved 2 tablespoons crumbs over top. Freeze until firm. Just before serving, garnish with sliced strawberries, if desired. Makes 6 to 8 servings.

CHOCOLATE-BANANA PIE

CRUST:

1⅓ *cups graham cracker crumbs*
½ *teaspoon cinnamon*
¼ *cup butter, melted*

In a small bowl mix together crumbs and cinnamon; stir in butter. Reserve 2 tablespoons crumb mixture. Press remaining crumbs firmly and evenly against bottom and sides of 9-inch pie plate. Bake in preheated 350°F. oven for 5 minutes. Cool.

FILLING:

2 *pints chocolate ice cream*
1 *cup mashed ripe bananas*

In a large mixing bowl beat ice cream until smooth; beat in bananas. Turn into crumb crust. Sprinkle reserved 2 tablespoons crumbs over top. Freeze until firm. Makes 6 to 8 servings.

It is important to keep the ice cream very hard between the several stages of preparation of this crêpe, so a good freezer is a must. The hot and cold combination has taste impact.

ICE-CREAM CRÊPES MELBA

    1 *pint pistachio or other ice cream*
    3 *tablespoons flour*
    1 *egg yolk*
    1 *whole egg*
    ¼ *teaspoon salt*
    ½ *teaspoon sugar*
    1 *cup milk*
    2 *tablespoons Grand Marnier liqueur*
       egg wash—of one egg beaten with 1 tablespoon water
    1 *to 1½ cups grated coconut*
       bland vegetable oil for frying
       Melba Sauce (page 94)

Form 8 ice-cream balls 2½ inches in diameter. Make a small hole about ¼ inch deep in center of each. Freeze on tray until firm. Blend flour, egg yolk, whole egg, salt, and sugar until smooth. Add milk, beat well and strain through a fine sieve. Set for 1 hour. Heat a 5- to 6-inch crêpe pan. Grease lightly with butter. Pour in 2 tablespoons of batter and rotate until lightly browned. Turn and brown slightly. Cool crêpes thoroughly. Fill ice-cream holes ¾ full with liqueur. Cover holes with soft ice-cream and refreeze. Rub edges of crêpe with egg wash and place ice cream ball in center. Fold crêpe around ball, enclosing it completely. Roll filled crêpe in egg wash, then in coconut. Return to freezer for 1 hour. Fill deep skillet to 3 inches of rim with vegetable oil. Heat to 350°F. Remove crêpes and plunge into oil for 20 seconds. Serve at once with Melba Sauce. Serves 8.

One of the finest restaurants in the world certainly has to be Horcher's in Madrid, where delectable food and exquisite service please the choosiest of patrons. Just imagine my intense pleasure when Manager Cristobal Prieto agreed to part with the recipe for this special dessert of the house. It's a taste knockout.

CRÊPES "SIR HOLDEN"

  6 *dessert crêpes (use recipe on page 229)*
  2 *tablespoons butter*
  1 *pint fresh strawberries, washed and hulled*
  2 *tablespoons sugar*
  1 *ounce Grand Marnier liqueur (orange-flavored liqueur)*
  1 *ounce brandy*
  1 *ounce Himbergeist liqueur (raspberry-flavored liqueur)*
1½ *cups whipped cream*
1½ *pints vanilla ice cream*

Prepare dessert crêpes as directed and set aside. (This may be done ahead of time. Stack crêpes between waxed paper and refrigerate until needed.) Melt butter in a skillet; add strawberries and sugar. Cook over very low heat for about 5 minutes, until strawberries are limp. Combine liqueurs and brandy; pour over strawberries and ignite to flambé berries. Shake pan to extinguish flames. Place ¼ cup whipped cream on each dessert plate; top with ½-cup scoop of ice cream. Dip each crêpe in strawberry sauce, then drape over scoop of ice cream. Spoon strawberry sauce over all. Makes 6 servings.

CHERRIES JUBILEE

MERINGUE GLACÉE AUX PÊCHES

      1   17-ounce can cling peach slices
    1½   tablespoons rum
    1½   tablespoons brandy
      4   egg whites
     ⅛   teaspoon cream of tartar
      1   cup sugar
    1¼   cups crisp chocolate cookies, crushed (15 2½-inch cookies)
     ¼   cup chopped almonds
    1½   quarts of coffee-flavored ice cream
     ¼   cup prepared chocolate fudge sauce
          whipped cream, optional

Drain peaches and sprinkle with rum and brandy. Set aside. Butter 8- or 9-inch pie plate and preheat oven to 325°F. With electric mixer, beat egg whites and cream of tartar until frothy; slowly add sugar, beating until very stiff and meringue makes glossy peaks. Gently fold in combined cookie crumbs and the chopped nuts. Spread over bottom and up side just to rim of pan, making bottom about ¼ inch thick and side 1 inch thick. Bake at 325°F. about 30 minutes. Cool away from drafts (don't worry if the meringue should fall in center, or cracks—it's supposed to behave that way). Fill cooled shells with ice cream. In spaces between ice cream, arrange peach slices. If Chocolate Sauce is thick, thin with liquid from marinated peaches. Dribble top with Chocolate Sauce and serve immediately. Serve with whipped cream, if desired. Or freeze pie and remove 5 minutes before serving. Makes 6 to 8 servings.

CHERRIES JUBILEE

> 1 *1-pound can sour pitted red cherries*
>   *water*
> ½ *cup sugar*
> 1 *teaspoon red food coloring*
> 1½ *tablespoons cornstarch*
> 1 *tablespoon butter*
> 2 *tablespoons brandy*
> 2 *tablespoons kirsch*
> ¼ *teaspoon almond extract*
>   *vanilla ice cream*

Drain cherries, reserving liquid. In saucepan, combine cherry liquid plus enough water to equal ¾ cup, sugar, and red food coloring. Cook over medium heat, stirring until mixture boils. Mix cornstarch with 2 tablespoons cold water and stir into hot liquid; add cherries. Heat until mixture boils and thickens. Cook 1 minute. Remove from heat; stir in butter, brandy, kirsch, and almond extract. Serve hot over vanilla ice cream. To flame, warm cognac (⅓ to ½ cup), ignite, and pour over sauce and ice cream. Makes 6 servings.

PEACH MELBA

    1 quart vanilla ice cream
    1 20-ounce can peach halves, drained and chilled
       Melba Sauce
       whipped cream

Spoon ice cream into 6 to 8 dessert dishes. Place drained peach halves, cut side down, on top of ice cream. Pour chilled Melba Sauce over peach halves. Garnish with whipped cream. Makes 6 to 8 servings.

    MELBA SAUCE:
    2 teaspoons cornstarch
    1 tablespoon water
    ½ cup light corn syrup
    ½ cup currant jelly
    1 10-ounce package frozen raspberries, thawed

Mix cornstarch, water, light corn syrup, currant jelly, and raspberries in small saucepan. Stirring constantly, bring to a boil over medium heat and boil 2 minutes. Remove from heat. Strain. Makes about 1¼ cups.

BANANA-APRICOT SUNDAE

    2   tablespoons sliced almonds
    2   tablespoons butter
    1½ teaspoons cornstarch
    1   8¾-ounce can apricot halves, drained and quartered
        apricot syrup
    2   tablespoons lemon juice
    ¼   cup Grand Marnier
    2   whole cloves
    1   cinnamon stick
    1   banana, thinly sliced
    1   pint vanilla ice cream

Brown almonds in butter; stir in cornstarch and apricot syrup. Add lemon juice, Grand Marnier, cloves, and cinnamon stick. Cook, stirring, until sauce thickens. Remove cloves and cinnamon stick. Stir in apricots and banana. Simmer 2 to 3 minutes or until hot. Spoon over ice cream. Makes 4 servings.

BRAZILIAN AVOCADO WHIP

>   2 large, fully ripened avocados
>   juice of 4 limes
>   ½ cup sugar
>   dash of salt
>   4 teaspoons instant coffee powder
>   green food coloring
>   2 pints vanilla ice cream

Dip cutting knife in lime juice; cut avocados in half. Remove pits and peel. Force through a sieve or food mill. Add lime juice, sugar, salt, coffee powder, and a few drops of green coloring. Combine mixture with softened ice cream and beat with rotary beater until smooth. Chill in freezing compartment of refrigerator just until whip becomes firm but not frozen. Stir mixture occasionally. Spoon into small dessert dishes and serve at once. Makes 6 to 8 servings.

CAFÉ AU RUM SUNDAES

CAFÉ AU RUM SUNDAES

> 1 29-ounce can cling peach slices
> 1 tablespoon cornstarch
> 1 tablespoon sugar
> 1 tablespoon instant coffee powder
> ¾ teaspoon rum extract
>   vanilla ice cream

Drain peaches, reserving 1 cup syrup. Combine cornstarch, sugar, and instant coffee in saucepan; blend in peach syrup. Cook and stir until mixture boils and is thickened. Add rum extract and peaches; heat through. Serve sauce warm over vanilla ice cream. Makes about 3 cups sauce.

While dining at the elegant Plaze Athénée in Paris, I tasted their Coupe Régence, which was making its debut on their menu. The chef was reluctant to part with the recipe for the cookie crust until it was further people-tested and proved popular. I loved it, and have included my version of the cookie with a softer and lacier texture. I offer you the American debut of a Paris original!

COUPE RÉGENCE

8 double-size Lace Wafer Cups (see page 101)
1 quart whole fresh strawberries
1 cup water
½ cup confectioners' sugar
½ cup sugar
1 tablespoon cornstarch
   red food coloring
1 quart pistachio ice cream
2 tablespoons slivered pistachios

Prepare the entire recipe for Lace Wafer Cups, using 2 tablespoons of the mixture for each wafer instead of one, thus making larger wafers. Instead of molding the wafers over the backs of custard cups, place them immediately into the tall stemmed coupe glasses to be used for this dessert, and finger them into graceful folds so that when cold they will have a fluted appearance. (The wafers will extend high above the rims of the glasses.)

Wash and stem berries. Sprinkle confectioners' sugar over 3 cups of the berries and let stand for an hour. Cook remaining cup of berries in water until soft; sieve berry pulp and juice. Sift sugar and cornstarch together; add to strawberry juice. Cook again, stirring until slightly thickened and clear. Add a few drops of red food coloring to get a deep rich red color, if the natural color seems pale. Arrange reserved 3 cups of berries in the wafers, and spoon thickened sauce over each berry. Chill.

When ready to serve, place a scoop of pistachio ice cream into the center of each wafer, permitting a ring of red strawberries to show around the edges. Stick slivers of pistachios into the top of each scoop of ice cream. Makes 8 servings.

FLAMING FRESH ORANGE SHERBET SHELLS

    2 *pints lemon or orange sherbet, slightly softened*
    5 *to 6 oranges, peeled*
    1 *to 1½ cups curaçao, white port wine, or ginger ale*
    6 *sugar cubes*
        lemon or orange extract

Line 6 champagne glasses or stemmed dessert dishes with about ¼ inch of softened sherbet, molding sherbet on bottom and up the sides of glasses with the back of a tablespoon to form a smooth even surface. (The edge may be smoothed with a table knife after sherbet is refrozen.) Freeze each shell immediately after molding. Cut oranges into bite-size pieces and drain. Place drained orange pieces in shallow glass dish; add curaçao or other liquid. Cover and chill thoroughly several hours. Just before serving, saturate sugar cubes with extract. Place frozen sherbet shells on serving tray. Spoon marinated oranges and small amount of liquid into each shell; top with sugar cube and ignite with match. Serve at once. Makes 6 servings.

RUM SHERBET

    3 *cups water*
    1 *cup light corn syrup*
    ¾ *cup sugar*
    1 *tablespoon grated lemon rind*
    1 *envelope (1 tablespoon) gelatin*
    ⅔ *cup lemon juice*
    ½ *cup rum*

Combine water, corn syrup, sugar, and lemon rind. Bring to a boil over medium heat, stirring constantly until sugar is dissolved. Then boil 5 minutes longer. Meanwhile soften gelatin in lemon juice; stir into hot mixture. Let cool, strain; add rum. Pour into two refrigerator trays, freeze

FLAMING FRESH ORANGE SHERBET SHELLS

with cold control set for fast freezing until mixture is almost firm, about 1½ hours. Turn into chilled bowl and beat with rotary beater or electric mixer until smooth. Return to tray. Freeze until firm, about 3 hours. Makes 14 servings.

7

Delightful Fruit Combinations

Nature has provided us with a sweet and delicious variety of fruits to dress up for dessert. Their color, texture, and taste give a perfect head start, while the methods in this chapter can elevate fruit to a sumptuous offering

Here again, how you serve may be as important as what you serve, if you want to excite the salivary glands of the diners at your table. So plan to use stemmed glassware where needed and elaborate individual bowls with self-saucers for the fruit-and-dumpling combinations. Ladle the fruit compotes at the table for maximum effect and cordiality.

Do pay particular attention to the directions that will indicate whether the dessert is to be served hot or cold, or a combination of both. Temperature, when serving fruit, can have a major influence upon the taste and satisfaction they are intended to have.

These recipes will be a welcome relief to any heavy meat menu, and many will appeal to a diet-conscious group. Fruit is the accessory of many recipes in other chapters, but here it is the star in its own right. With a little extra care in presenting it, you will bask in some well-earned applause.

PEARS IN LACE WAFER CUPS

      ½ cup light corn syrup
      ¼ cup lemon juice
      1 teaspoon grated orange rind
      8 small fresh pears, pared
      ¼ teaspoon almond extract
      8 Lace Wafer Cups
      3 tablespoons finely chopped almonds
         Fluffy Sabayon Sauce

Combine corn syrup, lemon juice, and orange rind in a 10-inch skillet. Bring to a boil. Add pears; cover and cook over medium heat, turning once, until the pears are just tender, about 5 minutes. Place pears in a bowl. Cook the remaining syrup until thickened, 3 to 5 minutes. Add almond extract. Pour over pears. Chill. Place Lace Wafer Cups in individual dishes. Cover bottoms of cups with chopped almonds. Fill each with some Fluffy Sabayon Sauce, then 1 well-drained pear, then more sauce. Makes 8 servings.

LACE WAFER CUPS:
      1 cup sifted flour
      1 cup chopped flaked coconut
      ½ cup light corn syrup
      ½ cup firmly packed brown sugar
      ½ cup butter or margarine
      1 teaspoon vanilla

Mix sifted flour and coconut. Combine corn syrup, brown sugar, and butter in heavy saucepan. Bring to a boil over medium heat, stirring constantly. Remove from heat. Gradually blend in flour-coconut mixture, then stir in vanilla. Drop 8 heaping tablespoonfuls onto foil-covered cookie sheet. (Drop remaining batter by scant teaspoonfuls to serve as cookies at another time.) Bake in a 350°F. oven for 8 to 10 minutes. Cool on a wire rack until foil may be peeled off easily, 3 to 4 minutes. Remove foil. Place cookies lace-side down on foil-covered cookie sheet and heat in a 350°F. oven 2 to 3 minutes. Remove from foil one at a time and place over inverted 5-ounce custard cups; press sides down to form cup. Cool a few minutes. Remove and cool completely on absorbent paper.

FLUFFY SABAYON SAUCE:

2 *tablespoons sugar*
1 *tablespoon cornstarch*
¼ *teaspoon salt*
1 *egg yolk, slightly beaten*
½ *cup milk*
½ *cup light cream*
2 *tablespoons sherry or brandy*
1 *egg white, stiffly beaten*

Combine sugar, cornstarch, and salt in the top of a double boiler. Mix in egg yolk thoroughly. Gradually add milk and cream. Cook over boiling water, stirring constantly, until mixture thickens, about 5 minutes. Remove from heat. Cool. Stir in sherry or brandy. Fold in beaten egg white. Chill.

APPLE-BERRY DUMPLING DESSERT

DUMPLINGS:

2 *tablespoons butter*
2 *cups canned applesauce*
½ *teaspoon salt*
½ *teaspoon lemon rind*
1 *tablespoon lemon juice*
⅓ *cup sugar*
2 *cups biscuit mix*
2 *tablespoons sugar*
¾ *cup light cream*
2 *cups blueberries*

Melt butter in a skillet or baking dish. Add applesauce, salt, lemon rind, lemon juice, and ⅓ cup sugar. Bake in a 350°F. oven for 15 minutes. In the meantime make dumplings by placing biscuit mix, 2 tablespoons sugar, and cream in a bowl. Mix with a fork until combined. Sprinkle blueberries over applesauce mixture. Drop batter from a tablespoon over fruit. Makes 5 or 6 dumplings. Return to oven and bake at 450°F. for 15 minutes or until dumplings are golden brown. Serve with Hard Sauce.

APPLE-BERRY DUMPLING DESSERT

HARD SAUCE:
¼ cup softened butter
1 cup confectioners' sugar
1 teaspoon vanilla

Cream ¼ cup butter and 1 cup confectioners' sugar. Beat until creamy. Beat in vanilla. Serve Hard Sauce over hot dumplings and fruit. Makes 5 or 6 servings.

If you are ever in Vienna, be sure to dine at the superb Stadt-krug Restaurant where Chef Bernhardt Mullhauser prepares his specialty of Curd Dumplings. Here is the recipe for you to try at home. Serve it with stewed plums to get the authentic Austrian flavor.

CURD DUMPLINGS WITH STEWED PLUMS
(Topfenknödel)

CURD DUMPLINGS:
1 pound farmer cheese
3 egg yolks
2 teaspoons powdered sugar
6 tablespoons butter, melted
½ cup very fine bread crumbs

Mash farmer cheese and combine with egg yolks and sugar. Form into 1½-inch balls. Drop into a large pot of rapidly boiling water; cook for about 15 minutes, or until dumplings rise to the top. Remove dumplings with a slotted spoon. Roll in melted butter and then in fine bread crumbs. Serve 2 dumplings to each person, and pass a small tureen of Stewed Plums. Makes about 12 servings.

STEWED PLUMS:
1 pound small, fresh dark plums, pitted and halved
1 cup water
1 cup sugar

Wash plums and cut in half; remove pits. Bring water and sugar to a boil; drop in plums and simmer until soft. Chill. Serve with above curd dumplings.

This is a spectacular fruit dessert when done from a chafing dish at the table. Or get a head start in the kitchen and bring it to the table to simmer and glaze, and then flambé.

MANDARIN BANANA FLAMBÉ

    2   tablespoons butter
    ½   cup sugar
    ½   cup Port wine
    ½   cup red currant jelly
    2   tablespoons slivered candied ginger
        grated rind and juice of ½ lemon
    6   bananas, cut in half lengthwise
    6   slices canned pineapple, drained
    2   11-ounce cans mandarin oranges, drained
    ¼   cup brandy, heated
    ¼   cup flaked coconut

Melt butter in a chafing dish or large skillet. Add sugar, wine, jelly, ginger, lemon rind, and juice to butter and stir until well blended. Add bananas (if too large, cut in half crosswise too), pineapple, and oranges and simmer 4 to 5 minutes, basting the sauce over the fruits to form a glaze. Just before serving, heat the brandy, pour over the fruits, and ignite. Sprinkle each serving with coconut. Makes 6 servings.

HOT FRUIT COMPOTE

1½ pounds mixed dried fruits, such as prunes, apricots,
    peaches, and pears
  cold water
1 cup sugar
1 tablespoon honey
2 tablespoons grated lemon rind
1 teaspoon cinnamon
¼ teaspoon nutmeg
3 tablespoons cornstarch
¼ cup orange liqueur

Cover dried fruits with cold water and let stand at room temperature for several hours, or overnight. Drain off water, and measure 1½ cups of it; pour into a saucepan or blazer pan of chafing dish. Add sugar, honey, lemon rind, cinnamon, and nutmeg. Bring to a boil and cook for 10 minutes. Mix cornstarch and orange liqueur together until smooth; stir into pan. Add drained fruits; stir until sauce is thickened and fruit is hot. To flambé, heat additional orange liqueur and pour over top of pan; ignite and shake pan until flames die out. Serve at once. Makes 8 servings.

PINEAPPLE AND FRUIT COMPOTE

1 ripe pineapple, pared, cored, and cut up
12 fresh apricots, pitted and halved
12 ripe plums, pitted and halved
2 large bananas, peeled and sliced
1 quart fresh red sweet cherries, pitted
1½ cups confectioners' sugar
½ cup sherry

Using a large container, combine all fruit. With a large serving spoon, fill the bottom of a glass compote bowl with a layer of the fruit mixture. Sift confectioners' sugar over the layer; continue to layer fruit and sift sugar until you have used up all the fruit and sugar. Then pour sherry over the top. Cover and refrigerate for at least 2 hours. Several times drain off the juice which accumulates and pour it back over the top of the fruit. Makes 8 servings.

GLAZED ORANGE AMBROSIA

> 6 large seedless oranges, peeled
> ¾ cup sugar
> ⅓ cup water
> ½ cup chopped walnuts
> ½ cup flaked coconut
> 3 tablespoons sherry wine

Slice oranges into ½-inch round discs; place in a large strainer over a bowl. Combine sugar and water in a saucepan; bring to a boil over high heat, stirring until sugar dissolves. Cook rapidly for 2 minutes. Pour hot syrup over the orange slices two or three times, allowing syrup to drain through the strainer, until all slices are thoroughly coated. Allow to drain a moment or two after final glazing. Toss with walnuts and coconut. Chill until ready to serve. Place in a serving bowl, or into individual sherbet glasses. Sprinkle with sherry and serve. Makes 6 servings.

Syllabub is traditionally a drink made of frothy milk and bubbling beer or wine—here it is made of light-as-air whipped cream combined with sherry wine, and a surprise of peaches underneath. Oh, if the pubs could see it now!

SYLLABUB

- 1 29-ounce can cling peach halves
- ½ cup sifted confectioners' sugar
- 1 cup whipped cream
- 1 egg white
- 3 tablespoons sherry wine

Drain peach halves. Slowly add half the confectioners' sugar to the whipping cream and whip until stiff. Beat egg white until soft peaks form; add remaining sugar and whip to stiff peak stage. Fold into whipped cream. Stir in sherry. Put peach halves in shallow bowl. Spoon cream mixture over the top; chill thoroughly about 1 hour before serving. Makes 6 to 8 servings.

RAISIN AND NUT BAKED APPLES

6 large baking apples
⅓ cup chopped walnuts
⅓ cup raisins
⅓ cup dark corn syrup
⅓ cup light cream

Core apples, making hole at least 1 inch in diameter. Place in shallow baking dish. Combine walnuts, raisins, corn syrup, and cream. Fill centers of apples with mixture. (Add leftover mixture while baking.) Bake in 350°F. oven until apples are tender, about 45 minutes. Serve with sauce. Makes 6 servings.

SAUCE:
1 cup light cream
⅓ cup dark corn syrup
3 tablespoons margarine
1 teaspoon vanilla
½ teaspoon cinnamon

Combine all ingredients in saucepan. Cook over low heat, stirring frequently, until thickened, about 30 minutes. Serve warm over apples. Makes about 1½ cups of sauce.

TAFFY APPLES

>   ¾ cup unsulphured molasses
>   ¾ cup sugar
>   ¾ cup water
>   ½ teaspoon cinnamon
>   ½ teaspoon nutmeg
>   ¼ teaspoon ground clove
>   ¼ teaspoon ginger
>   6 tablespoons lemon juice
>   8 large apples
>   whipped cream

In 10-inch skillet combine molasses, sugar, water, spices, and lemon juice; bring to a boil. Pare and core apples. Add to molasses mixture; cover and simmer 15 minutes. Uncover and simmer 30 minutes longer. Spoon syrup over apples frequently. Cool in syrup. Serve with whipped cream. Makes 8 servings.

TAFFY APPLES

FRESH STRAWBERRIES IN WINE

> 1 *quart fresh strawberries, washed and hulled*
> ½ *bottle chilled sauterne wine*
> 1 *cup heavy cream, whipped*
> *sprigs of mint, optional*

Cut strawberries in half lengthwise. Place in tall stemmed glasses. Pour sauterne wine over berries. Top with a dollop of whipped cream and garnish with mint, if desired. Makes 6 to 8 servings.

PEARS IN CLARET WINE

1 *cup water*
1 *cup sugar*
1 *cup claret wine*
4 *whole cloves*
8 *fresh pears, peeled*
   whipped cream, optional

Heat water and sugar together in a saucepan, until the sugar dissolves and becomes syrupy. Add wine and cloves, stir, and turn the heat low. Add whole peeled pears, and simmer until tender, about 15 to 20 minutes. Remove cloves. Chill pears in syrup. To serve, place all in one compote or in 8 individual serving dishes. Pass a sauceboat of whipped cream, if desired. Makes 8 servings.

8

Lovely Pies, Tarts, and Strudels

A pretty pie can catch the eye and set taste buds all aquiver. Which is reason enough to serve one or a selection of several for dessert.

Throughout most of the world, a PIE is a two-crusted dish encasing a filling of meat, fish, vegetables, fruit, or a fluffy combination of other ingredients. Sometimes the top crust is of meringue and the bottom crust of a crumb mixture. If it has one crust in Britain, it is a TART or a FLAN, but if it is a main-course pie in France it is a QUICHE, and in Italy it is a PIZZA. These can all be perched high on a cake stand or set into a silver-footed pie holder for better showmanship.

In America a PIE is anything in a pastry or crumb crust, or even anything set into a pie pan—one and two crusts included. A pie is sometimes called a TART here if it is one crusted and filled with an arrangement of glazed fruit. Tiny tarts are really TARTLETS and will be found in a later chapter.

STRUDEL originated in Austria and Hungary. It is com-posed of a thick, flaky pastry dough that is flattened, stretched into a large rectangle, filled with fruit, nuts, or cheese, and then rolled up into a long, thin tube. Strudel is baked in flat roasting pans and then cut crosswise for serving.

There are no plain old pies in the recipes that follow. In-stead, for elegance, there is a marvelous variety of intriguing combinations designed to be a credit to the hostess who cares about her culinary reputation.

Here's a switch—the meringue is baked underneath the lemon filling, instead of the usual way as a topping. Dollops of whipped cream finish off this picturesque pie.

MERINGUE-LINED LEMON PIE

CRUST:
1½ cups flour
  1 tablespoon sugar
  ½ teaspoon salt
  ½ cup shortening
  1 egg yolk, slightly beaten
  4 to 5 tablespoons water
  1 teaspoon vinegar

Sift flour, sugar, and salt into mixing bowl. Cut in shortening until the size of small peas. Combine egg yolk, water, and vinegar. Sprinkle over dry ingredients, a tablespoon at a time. Gently mix with fork until all dry ingredients are moistened. Form into a ball. Roll out on lightly floured board or pastry cloth to ⅛ inch thickness. Fit pastry into 10-inch pie pan. Trim and flute edge. Prick generously with a fork and bake in a 375°F. oven for 10 minutes.

MERINGUE LINING:
  1 egg white
  ¼ cup sugar
  ½ cup chopped pecans
  ¼ teaspoon vinegar

Beat egg white until soft mounds form. Gradually add sugar, beating until meringue stands in stiff, glossy peaks. Stir in chopped pecans and vinegar. Spread over partially baked crust and continue baking in a 375°F. oven for 10 to 15 minutes longer. Set aside to cool.

LEMON FILLING:
  1 envelope (1 tablespoon) unflavored gelatin
  ½ cup sugar
  ¼ teaspoon salt

6 *egg yolks*
½ *cup lemon juice*
¼ *cup water*
2 *teaspoons grated lemon rind*
6 *egg whites*
¾ *cup sugar*
½ *cup heavy cream, whipped*
   whipped cream for topping

Thoroughly mix gelatin, ½ cup sugar, and salt in a saucepan. Beat egg yolks with lemon juice and water; stir into gelatin mixture. Cook over medium heat, stirring constantly, until mixture just starts to boil. Remove from heat and stir in grated lemon rind. Chill, stirring occasionally, until mixture is very thick and forms mounds when dropped from spoon. Beat egg whites until soft peaks form; gradually add ¾ cup sugar, beating until stiff and glossy. Fold gelatin mixture and ½ cup cream, whipped, into egg whites. Pile into cooled, baked pastry shell. Chill until firm. Top with whipped cream dollops and garnish with grated lemon rind. Makes 6 to 8 servings.

ORANGE ANGEL PIE

MERINGUE SHELL:
3 *egg whites*
¼ *teaspoon cream of tartar*
¾ *cup sugar*
½ *cup finely chopped walnuts*

Beat egg whites with cream of tartar until foamy. Gradually add sugar and beat until mixture is very stiff and holds firm peaks. Fold in nuts. Spread over bottom and side of well-buttered 9-inch pie plate. Bake in a 275°F. oven for 1 hour. Cool completely.

ORANGE CREAM FILLING:
  1 envelope (1 tablespoon) unflavored gelatin
  ½ cup orange juice
  3 egg yolks
  ½ cup sugar
  ¾ cup milk, scalded
  1 teaspoon grated orange rind
  1 cup halved orange sections (3 oranges) *
  1 cup heavy cream, whipped
  2 teaspoons orange liqueur
  2 oranges, sectioned

Soften gelatin in orange juice. Beat egg yolks with sugar until thick and lemon colored. Scald milk and very slowly add to egg yolks, stirring constantly. Cook mixture over low heat until slightly thickened. Remove from heat, add orange rind and softened gelatin; stir until gelatin dissolves. Fold in orange sections, whipped cream, and orange liqueur. Chill until mixture will pile up; turn into cooled shell. Chill for 2 hours or longer. Serve garnished with orange sections. Makes 8 servings.

* To section oranges, cut slice from top, then cut off peel in strips from top to bottom, cutting deep enough to remove white membrane, then cut slice from bottom. Or cut off peel round and round, spiral fashion. Go over fruit again, removing any remaining white membrane. Cut along side of each dividing membrane from outside to middle of core. Remove section by section, over bowl to retain juice from fruit.

BUTTERSCOTCH CREAM PIE

CRUST:
  1⅓ cups graham cracker crumbs
  2 tablespoons sugar
  ¼ cup butter, melted

In a small bowl mix together crumbs and sugar; stir in butter. Press mixture firmly and evenly against bottom and sides of a 9-inch pie plate, building up slightly around rim. Bake in a preheated 350°F. oven for 5 minutes. Cool on wire rack.

FILLING:

 1 *envelope (1 tablespoon) unflavored gelatin*
 ¼ *cup cold water*
 3 *egg yolks, beaten*
 ½ *cup sugar*
 ½ *cup butterscotch pieces*
 ⅛ *teaspoon salt*
 1 *teaspoon vanilla*
 2 *cups cottage cheese, sieved*
 3 *egg whites*
 ½ *cup heavy cream, whipped*
 ⅓ *cup toasted flaked coconut*

Sprinkle gelatin on water to soften. In a small saucepan combine egg yolks, ¼ cup sugar, butterscotch pieces, salt, and softened gelatin. Cook over low heat, stirring constantly, until butterscotch pieces are melted. Add vanilla and cool; fold into cottage cheese. Beat egg whites until soft peaks form; add remaining ¼ cup sugar and continue beating until stiff. Fold into cottage cheese mixture; then fold in whipped cream. Chill until mixture mounds; turn into crust. Sprinkle coconut on top; chill. Makes 6 to 8 servings.

BUTTERSCOTCH CREAM PIE

FLUFF-FILLED CHOCOLATE PIE

CRUST:
  1 *cup sifted flour*
  ¼ *cup sweet cocoa mix*
  ¼ *teaspoon salt*
  ⅓ *cup shortening*
  3 *tablespoons milk*
  ½ *teaspoon vanilla*
  3 *drops red food coloring*
  ¼ *cup finely chopped pecans*

Sift together flour, cocoa mix, and salt. Cut in shortening until pieces are the size of small peas. Add milk, vanilla, and food coloring all at once. Stir into flour mixture until just moistened. Press into a ball, roll out between two sheets of wax paper. (Do not add extra flour.) Place in a 9-inch pie plate; make a fluted edge around the rim. Prick with a fork. Sprinkle with pecans; press nuts gently into bottom. Bake in a 400°F. oven for 10 minutes. Cool.

FILLING:
  1 *cup sugar*
  3 *tablespoons cornstarch*
  1 *envelope (1 tablespoon) unflavored gelatin*
  ¼ *teaspoon salt*
  1 *cup water*
  6 *egg yolks, beaten*
  2 *tablespoons grated lemon rind*
  ¼ *cup lemon juice*
  1 *tablespoon butter*
  6 *egg whites*
  3 *tablespoons sugar*
  1 *cup heavy cream, whipped*
    chocolate for garnish

Combine 1 cup sugar, cornstarch, gelatin, and salt in saucepan; blend in water. Cook over medium heat, stirring constantly, until thickened and bubbly. Slowly add a small amount of hot mixture to egg yolks, stirring constantly. Return to saucepan and cook for one minute longer. Remove from heat; blend in lemon rind, juice, and butter. Cool while beating egg whites. Beat whites until soft peaks form; add 3 tablespoons of sugar, one at a time, and continue beating until stiff. Fold egg yolk mixture gently into whites. Let chill for 30 minutes. Fold in whipped cream. Pour into cooled crust; sprinkle with shaved chocolate. Makes 6 to 8 servings.

Many of the recipes in this chapter have their own unique pie crust. The others call for plain pie crusts as in the following butter or shortening recipe. If you wish a richer and easier rolling crust, substitute half butter/half cream cheese for the amount of butter called for in the recipe.

PLAIN PIE CRUST

FOR ONE-CRUST PIE:
1 cup flour
½ teaspoon salt
⅓ cup butter or shortening
2 tablespoons cold water

FOR TWO-CRUST PIE:
2 cups flour
1 teaspoon salt
⅔ cup butter or shortening
4 tablespoons cold water

Combine flour and salt. Cut flour mixture and butter together until the particles are mealy in appearance. Add water and work dough until it is a soft ball. Roll each crust out on a floured board. Press into a 9-inch pie plate, fill, and cover with second crust if so desired in recipe. To bake a one-crust shell, prick with a fork and bake in a 375°F. oven for 12 to 15 minutes, or until lightly browned. Makes one or two 9-inch crusts.

PEACHY ORANGE CHEESECAKE PIE

CRUST:

1⅓ cups graham cracker crumbs
2 tablespoons sugar
¼ cup butter, melted

In a small bowl mix together crumbs and sugar; stir in butter. Reserve 2 tablespoons of crumbs for garnishing pie; press remaining mixture firmly and evenly against bottom and sides of a 9-inch pie plate, building up slightly around rim. Bake in preheated 350°F. oven for 5 minutes. Cool on wire rack.

FILLING:

1 envelope (1 tablespoon) unflavored gelatin
2 tablespoons water
½ cup sugar
1 egg, separated
½ cup frozen concentrated orange juice, thawed
1½ cups cottage cheese
½ cup heavy cream whipped
2 tablespoons sugar
sweetened sliced peaches

Soften gelatin in water. Meanwhile, in a 1-quart saucepan combine ½ cup sugar, egg yolk, and orange juice. Cook over medium heat, stirring constantly, until thickened (about 3 minutes). Remove from heat; add softened gelatin; stir until dissolved. Cool. In a large mixing bowl beat cottage cheese until smooth; beat in gelatin mixture; fold in whipped cream. In a small mixing bowl beat egg white until foamy; gradually add 2 tablespoons sugar and beat until stiff. Fold into cottage cheese mixture. Chill until mixture mounds. Mound into pie shell. Garnish top of pie with peach slices and reserved 2 tablespoons crumbs. Chill. Serve with sliced peaches. Serves 6 to 8.

*This pie is so orange that even the crust is flavored with it.
Refreshing and nutritious too.*

ORANGE CHIFFON PIE

FLAKY ORANGE PASTRY:

1½ cups sifted flour
  2 tablespoons sugar
 ½ teaspoon salt
 ½ cup shortening
  1 tablespoon grated orange rind
  3 to 4 tablespoons orange juice

Sift together flour, sugar, and salt. Cut in shortening with two knives or pastry blender until mixture resembles coarse meal. Mix in orange rind with fork. Gradually stir in orange juice; mix lightly. Lightly pinch dough together with fingers. Roll ⅛ inch thick; place in 9-inch pie dish and make fluted rim. Prick well with fork. Bake in 425°F. oven 10 to 12 minutes until lightly browned. Cool.

ORANGE CHIFFON FILLING:

  3 eggs, separated
 ½ cup sugar
  1 cup water
  1 3-ounce package orange flavor gelatin
 ¾ cup orange juice
  2 teaspoons grated orange rind
 ⅛ teaspoon salt

Combine slightly beaten egg yolks and ¼ cup of the sugar. In small saucepan bring water to a boil. Add a small amount of boiling water to egg-sugar mixture. Return mixture to boiling water; reduce heat to low and cook about 1 minute, stirring constantly. (Do not overcook.) Remove from heat. Pour over gelatin and stir until gelatin is completely dissolved. Add orange juice and rind. Chill until slightly thickened. Beat egg whites and salt until foamy. Add remaining ¼ cup sugar gradually, beating after each addition. Continue beating until mixture will stand in stiff peaks. Fold into slightly thickened gelatin. Turn into cooled pastry shell. Makes 6 to 8 servings.

FLUFFY PRUNE PIE

> 1 12-ounce box pitted prunes
> ½ cup dry sherry
> 2 envelopes (2 tablespoons) unflavored gelatin
> 1 cup cold water
> 1 cup sugar
> 4 tablespoons lemon juice
>   grated rind of 1 lemon
> 1 cup heavy cream, whipped
> 4 egg whites
> 1 baked 9-inch pastry shell (page 119)

Using scissors, snip prunes into slivers. Pour sherry over them to soak about 1 hour or until all sherry is absorbed. Let gelatin stand in cold water a few minutes and dissolve over hot water. To gelatin mixture, add ½ cup of the sugar and stir to dissolve. Stir in lemon juice and grated rind. Place in refrigerator until thickened but not set. When thickened, beat until foamy and fold in the slivered prunes and stiffly whipped cream. Now beat egg whites stiff but not dry and gradually beat in remaining ½ cup sugar until stiff peaks form. Finally, fold gelatin mixture into egg white mixture, folding gently until smooth. Turn into cooled 9-inch pastry shell. Chill in refrigerator several hours before serving. Makes 6 to 8 servings.

CARIBBEAN LEMON CHIFFON PIE

> CORN FLAKE CRUST:
> 1 cup corn flake crumbs
> ⅓ cup butter
> 2 tablespoons sugar

Measure corn flake crumbs, butter, and sugar into a 9-inch pie pan. Place in 350°F. oven 5 minutes. Remove from oven and mix thoroughly. Press against bottom and sides of pan. Chill.

CARIBBEAN LEMON CHIFFON PIE

LEMON CHIFFON FILLING:

2 *envelopes (2 tablespoons) unflavored gelatin*
1 *cup water*
3 *ice cubes equivalent to ½ cup water*
⅛ *teaspoon salt*
½ *cup unsulphured molasses*
1 *6-ounce can hard frozen lemonade concentrate*
1 *cup icy cold evaporated milk* *

Sprinkle gelatin on 1 cup of water in a 2½-quart saucepan to soften. Place over moderate heat, stirring constantly, until gelatin is dissolved, about 3 minutes. Remove from heat; stir in ice cubes, salt, and molasses. Stir in concentrate. When the concentrate is melted, the mixture should be slightly thickened. Whip chilled evaporated milk in small bowl of electric mixer until soft peaks form, about 2 minutes. Fold into gelatin mixture. Turn into crumb crust; chill until firm. Makes 6 to 8 servings.

* To chill evaporated milk, pour into ice-cube tray and freeze until soft ice crystals form around edge.

PUMPKIN PIE WITH ORANGE GLAZE

PUMPKIN PIE:
2 *cups canned cooked pumpkin*
¾ *cups firmly packed dark brown sugar*
2 *teaspoons cinnamon*
¾ *teaspoon salt*
¾ *teaspoon ginger*
½ *teaspoon nutmeg*
¼ *teaspoon mace*
⅛ *teaspoon ground cloves*
4 *eggs, slightly beaten*
1½ *cups light cream*
1 *unbaked 9-inch pie shell (page119)*

In a large bowl combine pumpkin and brown sugar. Add cinnamon, salt, ginger, nutmeg, mace, and cloves; blend thoroughly. Add eggs; gradually stir in light cream. Pour into pie shell and bake in preheated 400°F. oven 40 to 45 minutes or until a knife inserted off center comes out clean. Cool on wire rack. Spread with Orange Glaze.

ORANGE GLAZE:
¼ *cup sugar*
4 *teaspoons cornstarch*
   dash of salt
¼ *cup water*
2 *tablespoons grated orange rind*
¾ *cup orange juice*
1 *cup heavy cream, whipped*
   orange sections

In a 1-quart saucepan combine sugar, cornstarch, and salt. Gradually add water, then orange rind and juice. Cook over medium heat, stirring constantly, until thickened. Cook 2 additional minutes. Cool slightly. Spread carefully over baked pumpkin pie. Serve garnished with whipped cream and orange sections. Makes 1 cup.

FRENCH APPLE TART

PASTRY:
1 cup flour
2 tablespoons sugar
¼ teaspoon salt
½ cup sweet butter
1 egg yolk
1 tablespoon water
1 teaspoon grated lemon rind

Sift flour, sugar, and salt into a bowl. Cut in butter until mixture resembles coarse cornmeal. Add egg yolk, water, and lemon rind. Using fingers, blend until a smooth ball of dough is formed. Chill 1 hour. With floured fingers, pat evenly against bottom and sides of a 9-inch tart pan. Chill 1 hour before baking. Prick entire bottom and sides with tines of a fork. Bake in a preheated 350°F. oven for 10 minutes. Remove from oven.

FILLING:
3 medium apples, peeled and cored
¼ cup sugar
2 teaspoons lemon juice
¼ teaspoon ground cinnamon
⅔ cup apple jelly

Cut apples into thin slices about ⅛ inch thick (should measure about 3 cups). Combine apple slices, sugar, and lemon juice. Spread a thin layer of apples in partially baked pastry shell. Arrange remaining apple slices in slightly overlapping circles starting at outside edge and working toward center. Return to oven and continue baking for 35 minutes or until apples are tender and pastry is golden brown. Remove from oven and cool on a wire rack. Sprinkle top lightly with ground cinnamon. Heat jelly until melted, then spoon over apple slices. Before serving, let stand at room temperature or place in refrigerator until jelly sets. Makes 6 to 8 servings.

AUSTRIAN FRUIT TART

PASTRY:
2 cups flour
2 tablespoons sugar
2 egg yolks
2 teaspoons grated lemon rind
1 cup butter

Combine flour, sugar, egg yolks, and lemon rind. Add butter and work with fingers until a soft ball of dough is formed. With floured fingers, pat dough evenly against bottom and sides of a 12-inch pizza pan, making a fluted rim at edge of pan. Prick entire bottom with tines of a fork and bake in a preheated 375°F. oven for 15 to 20 minutes or until golden brown at the edges. Cool.

FILLING:
1 17½-ounce package frozen lemon or vanilla pudding, thawed
1 banana, sliced
2 navel oranges, peeled and sectioned
1 cup strawberries, hulled and quartered
1 small red apple, cored and cut into thin slices
1 cup seedless green grapes
4 apricots, peeled, pitted, and quartered
1½ cups apple or currant jelly

Spread pudding evenly in pastry shell. With a knife, mark top into 6 wedges. Fill each wedge with a different fruit. Melt jelly over low heat, stirring. Cool to lukewarm; spoon evenly over fruit. Chill several hours. Serve with or without whipped cream. Makes 10 to 12 servings.

AUSTRIAN FRUIT TART

Dining on the roof of the Hassler Hotel at the top of the Spanish Steps in Rome is one of life's pleasures. For me, another pleasure was to interview Chef Concari Gildo down in the immaculate hotel kitchen to find out how their famous Crostata di Frutta is prepared. Manager Nadio Benedetti kindly served as interpreter, as we spoke in two languages. But food has a language all its own.

CROSTATA DI FRUTTA

CRUST:
1⅓ cups butter
  1 cup sugar
  4 egg yolks
  4 cups flour
     grated rind of 1 lemon

Cream butter and sugar together; add egg yolks. Combine flour and grated lemon rind; gradually stir this into the batter until a dough is formed. Rest dough for one hour; then roll out and place in a 12-inch greased pan, patting dough up sides. Bake for 20 minutes at 400°F. Cool. Top with Crème and Fruit Topping. Makes 8 to 10 servings.

CRÈME:
  1 cup milk
  ⅓ cup sugar
  3 tablespoons flour
  2 egg yolks
  1 tablespoon cold milk

Scald milk. Combine sugar and flour; stir yolks and cold milk together and add. Gradually stir in scalded milk, and continue stirring until it is lump free. Pour into cooled crust. Top with Fruit Topping.

FRUIT TOPPING:
  1 ¼-inch thick by 12-inch round layer of sponge
     cake, optional
     canned fruit halves, such as peaches, apricots, etc.
     fresh berries, such as strawberries, blueberries, etc.

> ½ cup apricot jam
> 1 cup whipped cream

At this point a thin horizontal slice is cut off the top of a sponge cake used for another purpose, and placed over the crème. Thin slices of a plain cake would do, and the step may be omitted if you chill the crème before proceeding with the fruit arrangement.

Arrange fruit and/or berries in circles on top of the cake layer, or directly on top of the chilled crème. Heat jam and spread over top of fruit. Pipe whipped cream around the edges.

SPICY FRESH GRAPE PIE

> 1½ pounds fresh grapes (4 cups)
> 1 cup sugar
> ⅓ cup flour
> ¼ teaspoon salt
> ¼ teaspoon cinnamon
> ⅛ teaspoon nutmeg
> 1 tablespoon fresh lemon juice
> 2 tablespoons butter
> pastry for 2-crust 9-inch pie (page 119)
> vanilla ice cream

Halve grapes and remove seeds. In a large bowl mix sugar, flour, salt, cinnamon, and nutmeg. Add grapes and lemon juice; mix well. Line 9-inch pie plate with half of pastry; trim overhang to 1 inch. Roll out remaining pastry and cut into ¾-inch strips. Turn grape mixture into pastry-lined pie plate and arrange strips of pastry over top to make lattice pattern. Press ends of strips and pastry rim together and flute edge. Bake in a 450°F. oven 10 minutes; reduce heat to 350°F. and bake 25 minutes longer, until pastry is brown and grapes are tender. Serve warm or cool with vanilla ice cream. Makes 8 servings.

SPICY FRESH GRAPE PIE

RASPBERRY CUSTARD PIE

> 3 10-ounce packages frozen raspberries, thawed
> ¼ cup sugar
> 5 tablespoons cornstarch
> 1 baked 9-inch pastry shell (page 119)
> 1 cup heavy cream
> 2 teaspoons sugar
> ½ teaspoon vanilla

Drain juice from raspberries to yield 2½ cups. If necessary, add water. Combine ¼ cup sugar and cornstarch in small saucepan. Gradually blend in raspberry juice. Stirring constantly, cook over medium heat until mixture comes to boil and boils 1 minute. Cool to room temperature. Pour filling into pastry shell. Whip cream until soft peaks form when beater is raised. Gradually add 2 teaspoons sugar and the vanilla; whip until stiff peaks form when beater is raised. (Be careful not to overbeat.) Spread some cream around edge of filling to touch crust all around, then fill in center. Refrigerate about 2 hours before serving. Makes 6 to 8 servings.

APPLE-MINCEMEAT PIE

> 1 recipe pastry for double-crust pie (page 119)
> 1 1-pound jar prepared mincemeat
> 2 cups canned applesauce
> ½ cup light brown sugar
> 1 teaspoon lemon juice
> ½ teaspoon grated lemon rind
> 1 tablespoon butter

Combine mincemeat, applesauce, brown sugar, lemon juice, and rind. Mix well. Roll out half of pastry and line 9-inch pie pan. Pour in applesauce-mincemeat mixture. Dot with butter. Roll out remainder of pastry. Cut in strips and arrange lattice fashion over filling. Trim and flute pastry to make standing edge. Bake at 425°F. for 35 to 40 minutes or until golden brown. Serve warm or cold. Makes 6 to 8 servings.

PRUNE-APRICOT PIE

NUT PASTRY:
1 recipe pastry for double-crust pie (page 119)
¼ cup ground or grated blanched almonds
2 tablespoons sugar

Combine pastry with almonds and sugar. Roll out half of pastry and line 9-inch pie pan. Refrigerate until ready to fill. Reserve second half of pastry for lattice top.

For lattice top: Roll out remaining half of pastry between sheets of wax paper. Remove top sheet of paper, cut pastry in ½-inch strips. Leave pastry on paper and refrigerate until ready to use. This makes the delicate pastry strips much easier to handle.

PRUNE-APRICOT FILLING:
1 11-ounce package dried apricots
1 12-ounce package pitted prunes
3 cups cold water
1 tablespoon cornstarch
⅔ cup sugar
⅛ teaspoon salt
¼ teaspoon cinnamon
¼ teaspoon ginger
¼ teaspoon nutmeg
½ cup apricot-prune liquid
1 tablespoon lemon juice
1 tablespoon butter

Place apricots in saucepan, cover with cold water; bring to boil and simmer 5 minutes. Remove from heat and immediately add prunes. Stir and let stand about ½ hour. Drain fruit, reserving liquid. Combine cornstarch, sugar, salt, and spices in small saucepan; mix well. Gradually stir in ½ cup of fruit liquid. Cook, stirring constantly, until it boils and thickens. Stir in lemon juice and butter. Spoon fruit into pastry-lined pan. Pour syrup over. Arrange pastry strips lattice fashion on top. Seal edges. Bake in preheated 425°F. oven 25 to 30 minutes until crust is golden. Makes 6 to 8 servings.

WALNUT PIE

    3 eggs
    2 cups light corn syrup
    2 tablespoons margarine, melted
    1 teaspoon vanilla
    ⅛ teaspoon salt
    1 cup chopped walnuts
    1 unbaked 9-inch pastry shell (page 119)

Beat eggs slightly. Mix in corn syrup, margarine, vanilla, and salt, then nuts. Pour into unbaked shell. Bake in 400°F. oven for 15 minutes. Set oven temperature control at 350°F. and continue baking 30 to 35 minutes. (Filling should be slightly less set in center than around edge.) Makes 6 to 8 servings.

FROZEN PRALINE PIE

    ¾ cup light or dark corn syrup
    1 8-ounce package cream cheese, softened
    ¼ cup margarine
    ⅓ cup firmly packed light brown sugar
    ¾ cup milk
    1 baked 9-inch pastry shell (page 119)
    ¾ cup coarsely chopped or broken pecans

Gradually add corn syrup to cream cheese, stirring until smooth. Melt margarine and brown sugar over medium heat, stirring constantly. Gradually stir into cream cheese mixture. Stir in milk. Pour into baked shell. Sprinkle pecans over top of pie and freeze until firm, 4 to 6 hours. Makes 1 9-inch pie with 6 to 8 servings.

If you haven't tasted yams or sweet potatoes baked in a pie, you have a palate sensation ahead of you. Here are recipes you should be sure to try.

CRUNCHY YAM-APPLE PIE

 2 large tart apples
 1 tablespoon fresh lemon juice
 3 medium yams (about 1 pound)
 1 cup sugar
 1 teaspoon grated lemon rind
 1 egg
 2 tablespoons light cream
 1 unbaked 9-inch pastry shell (page 119)

Pare apples. Grate on coarse grater into a bowl. (There should be about 2 cups.) Stir lemon juice into apples. Pare yams. Grate on coarse grater into bowl with apples. (There should be about 3 cups.) Mix in sugar and lemon rind. Beat together egg and cream. Stir into apple-yam mixture. Turn into pastry shell. Bake in 350°F. oven 1 hour. Cool. Makes one 9-inch pie and serves 6 to 8.

YAM PRALINE PIE

 2 eggs
 ½ cup granulated sugar
 ½ cup packed light brown sugar
 1 teaspoon cinnamon
 ½ teaspoon nutmeg
 ½ teaspoon ginger
 ¼ teaspoon salt
 2 cups mashed cooked fresh yams
 ¾ cup milk
 1 cup light cream
 1 unbaked 9-inch pastry shell (page 119)

Beat eggs in mixing bowl; beat in granulated and brown sugar, spices, and salt. Blend in yams. Gradually stir in milk and cream. Pour into unbaked pastry shell. Bake in 400°F. oven for 10 minutes. Reduce heat to 350°F. and bake 20 minutes. Sprinkle Praline Topping over surface of pie. Continue baking 25 minutes or until knife inserted near center comes out clean. Cool completely before serving. Makes 6 to 8 servings.

PRALINE TOPPING:
⅓ cup chopped pecans
⅓ cup packed brown sugar
3 tablespoons soft butter

Mix all ingredients and sprinkle over surface of pie.

SWEET POTATO PEACH PIE

SWEET POTATO PEACH PIE

> 1 *cup flour*
> 1 *teaspoon salt*
> ⅓ *cup shortening*
> 2 *to 3 tablespoons cold water or milk*
> 1 *17-ounce can cling peach slices*
> 1 *cup cooked mashed sweet potatoes*
> 3 *eggs*
> ¼ *cup sugar*
> ¼ *teaspoon nutmeg*
> ¼ *teaspoon cloves*
> 1 *teaspoon cinnamon*
> 1 *6-ounce can evaporated milk, undiluted*
> ¼ *cup melted butter*
>   *whipped cream*

Mix flour and ½ teaspoon salt in bowl. Cut in shortening to consistency of coarse crumbs. Sprinkle with water; toss to moisten evenly. Shape into ball; roll pastry on floured surface to 11½-inch circle. Fit pastry into 9-inch pie pan; crimp edge. Drain peaches, saving ⅓ cup syrup. Reserve 6 to 8 peach slices. Mash remaining peaches and sweet potatoes together. Beat eggs; blend in sugar, spices, remaining salt, milk, butter, reserved peach syrup, and peach-sweet potato mixture. Pour into pastry shell. Bake in 375°F. oven 45 to 50 minutes. Garnish with whipped cream and reserved peach slices. Makes 6 to 8 servings.

It was thrilling to stand in the pastry kitchen of the Hotel Imperial in Vienna and watch several experienced chefs make light work of preparing many strips of this Viennese specialty. Once you have mastered the art of stretching strudel dough, you will marvel at how easy it is to make.

APPLE STRUDEL

STRUDEL DOUGH:

2 cups flour
1 egg
1 tablespoon fine cooking oil
  pinch of salt
½ cup warm water
  melted butter

Sift flour onto large pastry board. Make a well in the center of the flour. Add egg, oil, salt, and warm water to this well; with your fingers, work the flour into this well until all is a soft dough. Knead dough lightly but thoroughly. Place in a warmed bowl and cover with a clean towel. Allow dough to rest for one-half hour. Cover a large table with a clean sheet; sprinkle with flour and roll out the dough. Then place your hands, palm-side down, under the dough; with the backs of your hands stretch the dough until it becomes paper thin. (Flour the backs of your hands if necessary.) Brush the dough with melted butter and let it dry for about 10 minutes while you prepare the filling.

APPLE FILLING:

1½ pounds apples, peeled and sliced thin
¾ cup raisins
1 cup sugar
1 teaspoon cinnamon
1 cup fine bread crumbs
½ cup ground walnuts
2 tablespoons butter
  melted butter
  confectioners' sugar, optional

Combine sliced apples and raisins. Mix sugar and cinnamon through them. Combine bread crumbs and ground nuts; sprinkle thinly over the entire surface of the dough. Spread apple mixture along one long side of the dough. Dot with butter. Taking the sheet in your hands (or get another pair of hands to help for this step) on the side where you have placed the apples, roll the dough up. Place the seam-side down on a greased cookie sheet, or if it is too large bend it into a horseshoe shape. Pinch the ends of the dough closed and turn under. Brush the top of the strudel with melted butter. Bake in a 375°F. oven for 35 minutes or until lightly browned. Remove from oven and cool. Dust with sifted confectioners' sugar, if desired. Makes 10 to 12 servings.

APRICOT STRUDEL

> 1 recipe Strudel Dough (page 137, Apple Strudel)
> 2 1-pound cans apricot halves, drained
> 1 cup warmed apricot jam
> 1 cup slivered almonds
> 1 cup fine bread crumbs
> ½ cup ground almonds
> 2 tablespoons butter
>   melted butter
>   confectioners' sugar, optional

Prepare Strudel Dough as directed in recipe. Cut up apricot halves into smaller pieces; mix with apricot jam and slivered almonds. Combine bread crumbs and ground almonds; sprinkle thinly over the entire surface of the dough. Spread apricot mixture along one long side of the dough. Dot with butter. Follow directions for Apple Strudel and roll up. Brush with melted butter and bake in a 375°F. oven for 35 minutes or until lightly browned. Remove from oven and cool. Dust with sifted confectioners' sugar, if desired. Makes 10 to 12 servings.

CHERRY STRUDEL

> 1 recipe Strudel Dough (page 137, Apple Strudel)
> 1 pound sour cherries (dark Morella cherries are best), pitted
> ¾ cup sugar
> ½ teaspoon cinnamon
> ½ cup broken walnuts
> 1 cup fine bread crumbs
> ½ cup ground walnuts
> 2 tablespoons butter
> melted butter
> confectioners' sugar, optional

Prepare Strudel Dough as directed in recipe. Combine cherries, sugar, cinnamon, and broken walnuts. Combine bread crumbs and ground walnuts; sprinkle thinly over the entire surface of the dough. Spread cherry mixture along one long side of the dough. Dot with butter. Follow directions for Apple Strudel and roll up. Brush with melted butter and bake in a 375°F. oven for 35 minutes, or until lightly browned. Remove from oven and cool. Dust with sifted confectioners' sugar, if desired. Makes 10 to 12 servings.

9

Extravagant Cakes

Of all desserts, cake demands the closest attention to directions. But with the recipes in this chapter, if you can read—you can bake. You will find that many of the cakes get a head start with pantry products that make your preparation time shorter. Others are time-consuming European classics that are well worth your effort for special occasions. All are lavish and worthy of the pursuit of elegance.

Do read the recipe before starting to bake. Assemble all ingredients and utensils, taking into consideration the extra bowls and spoons you may need. Preheat your oven if a baking step is involved. Prepare the pan before starting the batter. The few minutes you spend in this way will save time and motion later on. If you find a word direction that is not clear to you, turn to the vocabulary chapter at the back of the book for clarification—in cakemaking, it does make a difference whether you "beat" or "fold."

To frost a cake on the serving platter, slip pieces of waxed paper under the edges to catch drips. Remove them when the frosting is set and save yourself a cleanup step. Be sure to let the cake cool properly before frosting, too, for best results.

Extravagant cakes are a grand finale to any meal, but they are particularly successful with an otherwise light dinner. Exercise your own sense of good taste at the menu-planning stage.

This can be baked in a tube pan, but is so much prettier when a bundt pan is used. They are now available in most housewares stores and can do double service with gelatin molds too. The secret to elegant desserts is to treat yourself first to good equipment.

SPICY APPLE BUNDT CAKE

  2 cups canned applesauce
  1 9-ounce package dried mincemeat
  2 packages active dry yeast
  ½ cup lukewarm water
  1 cup milk, scalded
  2 tablespoons sugar
  3 tablespoons shortening
  2 teaspoons salt
  1 cup nuts, finely chopped
  7½ to 8 cups sifted flour

Mix applesauce with crumbled mincemeat and cook until mixture is thick. Cool. Add yeast to lukewarm water. Let stand without stirring for 5 minutes. Stir yeast to blend well. Mix milk, sugar, shortening, and salt. Stir until shortening is melted. Cool to lukewarm. Stir in dissolved yeast and the nuts. Stir in apple-mincemeat mixture. Gradually beat in flour until a stiff dough is formed that can just about be stirred. Turn out on a lightly floured board and knead until dough is smooth and elastic. Put dough in a greased bowl, cover, and let rise in a warm place until double in bulk. Punch dough down and shape into a long roll, long enough to fit into a well-greased bundt pan or a 10- by 4-inch tube pan. Let rise until double in bulk. Bake in a 350°F. oven for 40 to 45 minutes or until cake when tapped sounds hollow. Cool on a rack. Spoon icing, on following page, over top. Makes 10 to 12 servings.

ICING:

    1   cup confectioners' sugar
    1½ teaspoons melted butter
    2   tablespoons cream
    ½   teaspoon vanilla

Combine confectioners' sugar, melted butter, cream, and vanilla. Spoon
this confectioners' sugar icing over the top.

The brand new Hotel Scandinavia in Copenhagen is a dazzling combination of spaciousness and plush comfort, as it soars into the skyline to become the greatest new hotel on the Scandinavian scene. The shining new kitchens boast of old-fashioned Danish desserts, such as this layered apple cake obtained from Head Chef Hans Lenz. Serve it with a dollop of sour cream for a taste delight.

DANISH APPLE CAKE

2 cups fine bread crumbs
4 tablespoons melted butter
¾ cup sugar
8 large apples
¾ cup white wine
1 tablespoon lemon juice
1 tablespoon sugar
½ teaspoon cinnamon
½ cup seedless raisins

Sauté bread crumbs in melted butter for a few minutes; stir in ¾ cup sugar and heat an additional few minutes, stirring constantly. Peel, core, and slice apples. Place apples in a saucepan with white wine, lemon juice, 1 tablespoon sugar, cinnamon, and raisins. Simmer apples in this mixture until almost tender; cool. Grease a 10-inch round pan. Place ⅓ of the bread crumb mixture over the bottom of the pan; then spread half of the apple mixture. Repeat the layers once more and top with a final layer of crumbs. Bake in a 275° oven for 30 minutes. Cool. Makes 12 servings.

This recipe may be used for a strawberry-topped cake by changing the ingredients of orange juice and rind to lemon. So if you have fresh strawberries on hand, try it that way.

ORANGE-BLUEBERRY SHORTCAKE

TOPPING:
⅔ cup sugar
2 tablespoons cornstarch
¼ teaspoon salt
½ cup water
3 cups fresh blueberries
2 tablespoons butter
1 teaspoon grated orange rind
2 teaspoons orange juice

In a 1½-quart saucepan combine sugar, cornstarch, and salt. Gradually add water, then 1 cup blueberries. Cook over medium heat, stirring constantly and mashing berries against side of pan until thickened. Cook 2 additional minutes. Add butter and stir until melted; stir in orange rind and juice and remaining 2 cups blueberries. Chill.

SHORTCAKE:
1¾ cups flour
⅓ cup sugar
1½ teaspoons baking powder
½ teaspoon baking soda
½ teaspoon salt
½ cup butter
1 tablespoon grated orange rind
½ cup orange juice
2 eggs, slightly beaten
3 tablespoons butter, softened
1 cup dairy sour cream

Into a bowl sift together flour, sugar, baking powder, baking soda, and salt. Cut in butter until it resembles coarse meal; add orange rind. Combine orange juice and eggs; add all at once to dry ingredients, stirring only until moistened. Spread evenly in a buttered 8-inch square cake pan. Bake in a preheated 400°F. oven for 20 to 25 minutes or until golden brown. Remove to wire rack to cool 3 minutes. Split horizontally; butter bottom half. Fold sour cream into blueberry mixture. Spread 2 cups on bottom cake layer; cover with top layer. Spoon remaining sauce over top. Serve immediately. Makes 9 to 12 servings.

APPLESAUCE GINGER LOG

1   15-ounce jar applesauce
⅔   cup sifted flour
1   teaspoon baking powder
1½ teaspoons ground ginger
½   teaspoon cinnamon
¼   teaspoon nutmeg
¼   teaspoon salt
4   eggs, separated
¾   cup sugar
¼   cup light molasses
½   teaspoon vanilla
    confectioners' sugar

Preheat oven to 375°F. Grease a 15- by 10- by 1-inch jelly roll pan. Line with waxed paper, grease again. Pour applesauce into pan; spread evenly. Sift dry ingredients; set aside. Beat egg whites until soft peaks form. Gradually add sugar, beating until stiff. In a small bowl, beat egg yolks until thick and lemon colored. Add molasses and vanilla and beat until very well combined. With a wire whisk or rubber spatula, fold egg yolk mixture and dry ingredients into beaten egg whites, just until combined. Pour batter over applesauce, spread to cover completely. Bake 15 to 18 minutes until golden. Let cake stand 5 minutes. Turn out, apple-side up, on a towel sprinkled with confectioners' sugar. Gently lift off waxed paper. Roll cake up at once lengthwise, using the towel to turn it. Serve with Applesauce Ginger Whip Topping. Makes 8 to 10 servings.

APPLESAUCE GINGER WHIP TOPPING:

 1 *cup applesauce*
 ¼ *teaspoon ginger*
   dash of cinnamon
 1 *cup prepared whipped cream or topping*

Fold applesauce, ginger, and cinnamon into prepared whipped cream or topping. Makes about 2 cups.

ORANGE ROLL CAKE

 3 *eggs*
 1 *cup sugar*
 5 *tablespoons orange juice*
 1 *cup sifted cake flour*
 1 *teaspoon baking powder*
 ¼ *teaspoon salt*
 1 *teaspoon freshly grated orange rind*
   whipped cream

In large mixer bowl, beat eggs until very thick and light; gradually beat in sugar, then orange juice. Sift together dry ingredients; add to egg mixture and beat just until smooth. Stir in orange rind. Pour into a 15½- by 10½- by 1-inch jelly roll pan that has been lined with waxed paper greased on both sides. Bake in a 375°F. oven for 12 to 15 minutes, or until cake tests done. Gently loosen edges with spatula; turn out onto towel that has been dusted with powdered sugar. Roll up cake with towel, starting at narrow edge; cool thoroughly on rack. Unroll cooled cake; spread with cooled Orange Filling, then roll up again. Slice, and serve with a dollop of whipped cream. Makes 8 to 10 servings.

ORANGE FILLING:

 1 *cup sugar*
 ¼ *cup cornstarch*
 ½ *teaspoon salt*
 1 *tablespoon grated orange rind*

>   1   *cup orange juice*
>   1½   *tablespoons lemon juice*
>   2   *tablespoons butter*

In saucepan, thoroughly combine sugar, cornstarch, and salt; blend in remaining ingredients until very smooth. Bring to a boil over medium heat, stirring constantly; boil 1 minute. Cool thoroughly before spreading on Orange Roll Cake.

ORANGE ROLL CAKE

SOUTHERN GENTLEMAN'S CAKE

LAYERS:

2 *cups sifted flour*
½ *teaspoon cream of tartar*
1½ *teaspoons baking powder*
8 *eggs, separated*
2 *cups sugar*
grated rind and juice of 1 lemon
dash salt
1 *cup Concord grape jelly*

Sift together flour, cream of tartar, and baking powder. Beat egg yolks until very thick and lemon colored, about 5 minutes. Gradually add sugar and continue beating until mixture is smooth and pale yellow. Stir in lemon rind and juice. In a clean bowl, beat egg whites with salt until stiff peaks form. Gradually fold egg whites and flour into egg yolk mixture. Pour into 2 greased and floured 9-inch square cake pans. Bake at 325°F. for 30 minutes or until cake begins to pull away from the sides of pan. Loosen edges from pan and turn out onto cake racks to cool. When layers are cool, split each in half crosswise. Spread Concord grape jelly between the layers.

FROSTING:

¼ *cup butter*
6 *cups unsifted confectioners' sugar*
1 *egg yolk*
2 *tablespoons lemon juice*
3 *to 4 tablespoons orange juice*
grated rind of 1 orange
grated rind of 1 lemon
candied violets or candied fruit slices, optional

Cream butter; gradually beat in confectioners' sugar, egg yolk, and lemon juice. Beat in enough orange juice to give good spreading consistency. Stir in orange and lemon rind. Frost sides and top of cake. Garnish with candied violets or candied fruit slices, if desired. Makes 10 servings.

At that jewel of elegant hostelries, the Excelsior Hotel in Florence, Manager Piero Modena gallantly translated while Chef Egidio Alzetta demonstrated how he prepares his famous Zuccotto. Then we tasted. Mmmmmm!

ZUCCOTTO

1 *cooled baked 8-inch sponge cake layer*
2 *cups heavy cream, whipped*
1 *square semisweet chocolate, cut up fine*
½ *cup cocoa*
½ *cup maraschino cherry juice*
   maraschino cherries, optional

Trim brown edges from sponge cake. Cut cake into ¼-inch-thick strips. Line a 4-cup round bowl with the strips of cake, until the bowl is completely lined. Trim off any pieces that stick up over the top of the bowl and use them to fill in any gaps in the bowl. Spread 1½ cups of whipped cream over the cake liner, making a layer about 1-inch thick. Sprinkle that layer with finely cut chocolate. Combine cocoa with 1½ cups whipped cream. Pour this mixture into the center of the bowl. Use the remaining whipped cream to fill in the top. Then place additional strips of sponge cake over the top of the bowl, touching along the sides; trim at the edges. Freeze for at least 3 hours. Before serving, invert bowl and remove Zuccotto. Brush maraschino juice all over sponge cake exterior. If desired, pipe additional whipped cream in several swirls on top and decorate with cherries. Cut in wedges. Makes 8 servings.

On a visit to the Instituto Professionale Alberghiero, a unique hotel management school in Florence, Italy, I was pleased to acquire the recipe for "Gâteau Fedora" from Master Chef Alberti Pasquale and Pastry Chef Otello Ferroni. It is typical of Florentine desserts, with layers of cake, custard, whipped cream, and chocolate, combined into a mouth-watering temptation.

GÂTEAU FEDORA

SPONGE CAKE:

   5 eggs, separated
1¼ cups sugar
1½ tablespoons lemon juice
1¼ cups flour
   1 teaspoon baking powder
      pinch of salt

Beat egg yolks until lemon colored. Add sugar and beat. Add lemon juice. Combine flour, baking powder, and salt; sift into batter. Beat egg whites until stiff; fold into batter. Pour mixture into a greased and floured 10-inch round layer pan. Bake in a 350°F. oven for 30 to 40 minutes, or until firm and lightly browned. Remove from oven, invert pan on a cake rack, and let cake hang in pan until cool. Then carefully cut out center of the cake, leaving a solid rim and base for the filling.

CREAM FILLING:

1½ cups milk
   ½ cup sugar
4½ tablespoons flour
   3 egg yolks, slightly beaten
   1 teaspoon vanilla

Scald milk. Combine sugar and flour in top of a double boiler; stir in egg yolks and vanilla, mixing well. Stir in several tablespoons of the scalded milk. Gradually stir the scalded milk into this mixture, then cook over water until thickened and smooth. Cool. Pour into center of sponge cake.

TOPPING:
1 *cup heavy cream*
3 *tablespoons sugar*
    sweet chocolate bar
    confectioners' sugar

Whip cream until soft peaks form; gradually add sugar and whip until stiff. Pile over custard Cream Filling in a mounded dome with a smooth surface. Make large curls of chocolate with a vegetable peeler; scatter over surface of cake. Top chocolate curls with a light sifting of confectioners' sugar. Chill until serving time. Makes 12 to 14 servings.

STRAWBERRY GÂTEAU

1¼ *cups sifted flour*
 ¾ *cup sugar*
 ¼ *cup cornstarch*
  2 *teaspoons baking powder*
 ½ *teaspoon salt*
 ½ *cup corn oil*
 ½ *cup water*
  2 *eggs, separated*
 ½ *pint heavy cream*
  1 *pint strawberries*
      confectioners' sugar

Grease two 8-inch layer cake pans and line bottoms with waxed paper. Sift flour, sugar, cornstarch, baking powder, and salt together into mixing bowl. Combine corn oil, water, and egg yolks. Add to dry ingredients and beat until smooth. Beat egg whites until peaks form. Fold into batter. Pour into prepared pans. Bake in a 400°F. oven until lightly browned and firm, about 25 to 30 minutes. Cool. Whip cream. Spread about ¾ of the cream on one cake layer. Pile all but 6 strawberries on top of this layer, covering 2 sides only and leaving a wide strip down the middle uncovered. Cut second cake layer in half and place on top of cake, slightly raised at sides, to form wings. Pipe remaining cream down the center, then cover with reserved 6 berries. Dust wings lightly with confectioners' sugar. Makes 6 to 8 servings.

STRAWBERRY-ORANGE BUTTER CAKE

½ cup butter
1½ cups sugar
2 eggs
½ teaspoon almond extract
2½ cups sifted cake flour
2½ teaspoons baking powder
½ teaspoon cinnamon
¼ teaspoon salt
¼ teaspoon nutmeg
⅛ teaspoon ginger
1 cup milk

Butter bottoms of two 9-inch cake pans and dust with flour; set aside. In a mixing bowl cream butter; gradually add sugar and beat until light and fluffy. Beat in eggs, one at a time. Add almond extract. Sift together flour, baking powder, cinnamon, salt, nutmeg, and ginger. Add to creamed mixture alternately with milk, beginning and ending with dry ingredients. Divide evenly into pans. Bake in a preheated 350°F. oven 25 to 30 minutes. Cool in pans on wire racks 10 minutes. Turn onto racks and cool completely. Frost and fill with Orange Sauce Frosting. Makes 10 to 12 servings.

ORANGE SAUCE FROSTING:
6 tablespoons sugar
6 tablespoons flour
⅛ teaspoon salt
1½ cups fresh orange juice
1 egg, slightly beaten
1 teaspoon grated orange rind
¾ cup butter
¾ cup confectioners' sugar
½ teaspoon almond extract
1 pint sweetened sliced fresh strawberries, drained

In a 1-quart saucepan combine sugar, flour, and salt; gradually stir in orange juice. Cook over medium heat, stirring constantly, until thickened. Cook 2 additional minutes. Blend small amount of hot mixture into

STRAWBERRY-ORANGE BUTTER CAKE

egg; return all to saucepan. Cook, stirring constantly, 1 additional minute. (Do not boil.) Remove from heat; add orange rind. Press a circle of
waxed paper over surface of filling to prevent drying as it cools. Chill. In
a small mixing bowl cream butter; gradually add confectioners' sugar and
beat until light and fluffy. Add almond extract. Beating constantly, add
orange mixture, a small amount at a time, beating just until blended.

To assemble cake: Place bottom cake layer on plate; spread ½ cup
frosting on first layer. Spread 1½ cups strawberries over this in single
layer. Spread ½ cup frosting on bottom of second layer and place this
frosted side on strawberries. Spread remaining frosting on top and sides
of cake. Garnish with remaining sweetened strawberries.

Some people shy away from a recipe containing yeast, simply because it sounds difficult to use. It's really very easy and takes just a little extra effort to knead the dough well and be around to watch it rise in a warm place. Here's a chance to use your electric warming tray, if you wish. Set it on very low and keep the bowl out of a draft. Be sure to have a good quality of rum handy before you start—some goes onto the cake, and a bit may go into the cook.

BABA AU RUM WITH APRICOT GLAZE

    1¾ to 2¼ cups unsifted flour
    ¼ cup sugar
    1 package dry yeast
    ½ cup milk
    ¼ cup butter
    3 eggs (at room temperature)
       Rum Syrup
       Apricot Glaze

In a large bowl, thoroughly mix ⅔ cup flour, sugar, and undissolved dry yeast. Combine milk and butter in a saucepan. Place over low heat until liquid is warm (butter does not have to melt completely). Gradually add to dry ingredients and beat 2 minutes at medium speed of electric mixer, scraping bowl occasionally. Add eggs and ½ cup flour; beat 2 minutes at high speed, scraping bowl occasionally. Stir in enough additional flour to make a thick batter. Cover; let rise in warm place, free from draft, until bubbly, about 1 hour. Stir down batter. Turn into a well-greased and floured 2-quart tube-shaped baking pan. Cover; let rise in warm place free from draft 30 minutes. Bake in a preheated moderate oven 350°F. for 30 to 35 minutes or until done. Remove from pan and cool on wire rack for 15 minutes; return to pan. Prick top with fork. Gradually pour hot Rum Syrup over cake until all the syrup is absorbed. Let stand 30 minutes or longer. When ready to serve, reheat cake in pan in a 300°F. oven for 15 minutes or until heated. Invert cake onto a serving platter. Spoon part of the hot Apricot Glaze over the cake and pass the remaining portion separately for spooning over each serving. To serve flaming, heat 2 tablespoons of rum in a large ladle. Ignite rum; stir it into the hot Apricot Glaze and while flaming, spoon the mixture over the cake. Makes 10 to 12 servings.

RUM SYRUP:

1 *cup sugar*
½ *cup water*
½ *cup light rum*
¼ *cup orange juice*

Combine sugar and water in a saucepan. Cook, stirring constantly, until sugar is dissolved. Simmer 10 minutes. Remove from heat; stir in rum and orange juice.

APRICOT GLAZE:

1 *cup apricot preserves*
1 *tablespoon lemon juice*
2 *tablespoons light rum*

Heat apricot preserves in a small saucepan until melted. Stir in lemon juice and rum.

Recently I visited the beautiful Mullets Bay Beach Hotel on the island of St. Maartin in the Caribbean. One look at the dessert buffet table made me realize that I was on a busman's holiday, for it was an array that only an experienced pastry chef could produce. Next morning I managed to find German-trained Hartmut Trager in his separate baking quarters, just in time to find him preparing a Bienenstich (Bee's Sting) cake, named for its honey topping. It has an intriguing taste created by the unexpected cinnamon in the honey!

BIENENSTICH

SOUR CREAM YEAST DOUGH:
2½ cups flour
¼ cup sugar
½ teaspoon salt
2 packages active dry yeast (do not use cake yeast for this method
2 teaspoons grated lemon rind
¼ cup milk
½ cup dairy sour cream
¾ cup butter
2 eggs, beaten
1 teaspoon vanilla

Pour 1 cup of the flour into a large mixing bowl; add sugar, salt, active dry yeast, and grated lemon rind. In a small saucepan, pour milk, sour cream, and cut up pieces of butter; heat and stir until very warm and butter is almost completely melted. Remove from heat and pour gradually into the flour mixture; beat for 2 minutes at medium speed with an electric mixer. Add beaten eggs. Add vanilla. Then gradually add the remaining 1½ cups of flour. Beat at high speed for 2 minutes more. Turn into a greased 10-inch spring form pan; cover with a clean towel, and put in a warm place to double in bulk, about 1 hour. When doubled, make the topping.

HONEY TOPPING:

2 *tablespoons water*
1 *cup sugar*
½ *pound butter*
2 *tablespoons honey*
1 *tablespoon cinnamon*
8 *ounces coarsely chopped almonds*

In a large skillet, pour the water and sugar; stir to dissolve. Place over heat and stir until sugar begins to caramelize and turn lightly brown. Add pieces of butter, stirring constantly. Remove from heat; stir in honey, cinnamon, and almonds.

With knuckles, punch dough down halfway. Immediately spoon topping over the entire surface. Let rise again for 20 minutes. Bake in a preheated 350°F. oven for about 30 minutes. Remove from oven and cool.

FILLING:
1 *recipe Cream Filling (page 197, Saint-Honoré Torte)*

Remove side of spring form. Split cake in half and fill with Cream Filling. Makes 12 to 14 servings.

The cuisine at the Hotel Meurice in Paris is as deluxe as the accommodations, which overlook the Tuileries Gardens just a short walk from the famous Louvre. Maître d'Hôtel Otto Sternig claims that Savarin Belle Fruitière, as prepared by Chef Lucien Chassignat, is their most popular dessert. After one taste, I could not help but wheedle the recipe for you.

SAVARIN BELLE FRUITIÈRE

   ½ *cup milk*
   1 *teaspoon salt*
   ½ *ounce yeast*
   2 *eggs, beaten*
   2 *cups flour*
   ½ *cup butter*
     grated rind of 1 lemon
1½ *tablespoons sugar*
   2 *egg yolks*
   1 *cup water*
   ½ *cup sugar*
   ½ *cup rum*
   3 *cups drained fruit salad (fresh cut-up apples, pineapple, cherries, strawberries, etc.)*

Scald the milk; dissolve the salt and yeast in the milk. Stir in the two beaten eggs, and then the flour. Cover bowl with a clean towel and let dough rise to double its bulk. When this has happened, cream the butter; add grated lemon rind and 1½ tablespoons of sugar. Beat well and then add egg yolks. Blend this mixture into the yeast dough. Then put the dough into a greased circular tin about 12 inches across with a large hole in the middle. Let dough rise once more. When the dough has risen up to the brim of the tin, put it in the oven and bake at 350°F. for about 35 minutes or until medium browned and beginning to shrink away from the side of the tin. Cool for a few minutes, then turn over on a rack and remove from tin.

In a saucepan, heat the water and ½ cup sugar together to the boiling point; remove from heat and stir to be sure that sugar has dissolved. Then cool it a bit and stir in ¼ cup of the rum.

Prick the top of the warm savarin in several places with a fork; then slowly pour this Rum Syrup over the top so it will be absorbed. Place savarin on a serving platter when ready to serve; fill the center of the ring with drained fruit. Pour the remaining ¼ cup of rum over the top and ignite if you wish. Serve at once. Makes 10 to 12 servings.

If there's a choco-holic in your house, this is the cake to bake. It's a chocolate lover's day dream.

CHOCOLATE CAKE WITH MOCHA FROSTING

      ½ cup butter
    1½ cups sugar
      4 eggs, separated
      1 teaspoon vanilla
      2 1-ounce squares unsweetened chocolate
      5 tablespoons water
    1¾ cups sifted flour
      2 teaspoons baking powder
      ½ cup milk

Generously butter bottoms of two 9-inch round cake pans and dust with flour. In a mixing bowl cream butter; gradually add sugar and beat until light and fluffy. Beat in egg yolks. Blend in vanilla. In a small saucepan heat chocolate and water. Stir until melted and mixture becomes smooth and thickened. Add to creamed mixture. Sift together flour and baking powder; add to creamed mixture alternately with milk, beginning and ending with dry ingredients. Beat egg whites to soft peak stage; fold into chocolate batter. Divide evenly into pans. Bake in a preheated 350°F. oven for 25 to 30 minutes. Cool in pans on wire racks for 5 minutes. Then turn onto racks and cool completely. Fill with Milk Chocolate Filling and frost with Mocha Fluff Frosting. Makes 10 to 12 servings.

MILK CHOCOLATE FILLING:

- ½ cup sugar
- ¼ cup flour
- 1 1-ounce square unsweetened chocolate, cut up
- ¼ teaspoon salt
- 1½ cups milk
- 2 egg yolks, slightly beaten
- 1 teaspoon vanilla

In a 1-quart saucepan combine sugar, flour, chocolate, and salt; gradually stir in milk. Cook over medium heat, stirring constantly, until thickened. Cook for 2 additional minutes. Stir a little of hot mixture into egg yolks; return to pan. Cook for 1 minute. (Do not boil.) Add vanilla. Cool completely before spreading. This makes filling for a 2-layer, 9-inch cake.

MOCHA FLUFF FROSTING:

- 6 tablespoons butter
- 2 teaspoons instant coffee powder
- ¾ cup sifted confectioners' sugar
- 3 1-ounce squares unsweetened chocolate, melted and cooled
     dash of salt
- 1 teaspoon vanilla
- 2 egg whites
- ¾ cup sifted confectioners' sugar

In a mixing bowl cream butter; gradually add ¾ cup confectioners' sugar and beat until light and fluffy. Blend in chocolate, salt, and vanilla. Beat egg whites to soft peak stage; gradually add remaining sugar, beat until stiff. Gently fold chocolate mixture into egg whites. This makes frosting to spread on top and sides of 2-layer, 9-inch round cake.

CHOCOLATE CAKE WITH MOCHA FROSTING

SWEET CHOCOLATE LOAF

    1 4-ounce package sweet cooking chocolate, broken in pieces
    ¼ cup water
    ⅓ cup butter
    ¾ cup sugar
    2 egg yolks
    ½ teaspoon salt
    ½ teaspoon vanilla
    ½ teaspoon baking soda
    ½ cup buttermilk
    1¼ cups sifted flour
    2 egg whites

Melt chocolate with water in small saucepan over low heat, stirring until smooth. Cool. Cream butter; gradually add sugar. Continue creaming for about 3 more minutes. Add egg yolks, salt, vanilla, and chocolate mixture. Beat until well blended—about 2 minutes. Dissolve soda in buttermilk; add to egg mixture alternately with flour, beginning and ending with flour. Beat egg whites until soft shiny peaks form. Fold into batter. Pour into 15- by 10-inch jelly roll pan which has been lightly greased and lined on the bottom with waxed paper. Bake at 350°F. for 15 to 18 minutes, or until cake just begins to pull away from sides of pan. Cool in pan 5 minutes. Turn out on wire rack. Remove paper and finish cooling.

Mark the long side of the cake into 3 equal portions (about 5 inches each); cut to form 3 layers. Set one layer of cake, top-side up, on a plate. Spread with about ¾ cup of whipped cream filling and sprinkle with about 2 tablespoons toasted coconut. Repeat, making another layer with filling; and then spread remainder of filling over the top. Sprinkle with remaining coconut. Do not frost sides of cake. Makes 10 servings.

    FILLING AND TOPPING:
    1 cup heavy cream
    2 tablespoons sugar
    ½ teaspoon vanilla
    ¼ cup chopped pecans
    ⅓ cup flaked coconut, toasted

Combine cream and 2 tablespoons sugar; whip just until soft peaks will form. Fold in vanilla and nuts. Fill and frost as directed.

CHOCOLATE-MOLASSES CAKE

        2⅓ cups sifted flour
          2 teaspoons baking powder
          ½ teaspoon baking soda
          ½ teaspoon salt
          ½ cup sugar
          ½ cup shortening
          ¾ cup milk
          ¾ cup unsulphured molasses
          2 eggs
          2 1-ounce squares unsweetened chocolate, melted and
                slightly cooled

Sift flour, baking powder, baking soda, salt, and sugar into large bowl of electric mixer. Add shortening, milk, and ½ cup of the molasses. Blend at low speed, then beat at medium speed 2 minutes. Add remaining ¼ cup molasses, eggs, and chocolate. Beat at medium speed 2 minutes longer. Turn into 2 well-greased 9-inch pans. Bake in 350°F. oven, 25 to 30 minutes. Frost with Taffy Frosting. Makes one 9-inch cake. Serves 8 to 10.

        TAFFY FROSTING:
          2 egg whites
          ¼ cup water
          1 cup sugar
          2 tablespoons unsulphured molasses
          ⅛ teaspoon salt
          ½ teaspoon vanilla

Combine egg whites, water, sugar, molasses, and salt in top of double boiler. Beat over rapidly boiling water with rotary or electric beater until frosting stands in peaks. Remove from heat; add vanilla. Makes filling and frosting for 9-inch layer cake.

MOLASSES CAKE

        1 cup butter
     1½ cups sugar
        3 eggs
        ¾ cup unsulphured molasses
     3¾ cups sifted flour
        ¾ teaspoon soda
        ¾ teaspoon salt
        3 teaspoons cinnamon
     1½ teaspoons cloves
        1 teaspoon nutmeg
        ¾ cup buttermilk

Cream butter; slowly add sugar. Add eggs and beat until light and fluffy. Blend in molasses. Sift together flour, soda, salt, and spices; add to mixture alternately with buttermilk. Turn into greased 10-inch tube pan. Bake in 325°F. oven for about 1 hour, or until cake tests done. Cool on wire rack. Serve with Lemon Topping. Serves 8 to 10.

        LEMON TOPPING:
        2 tablespoons cornstarch
        ½ cup sugar
        ¼ teaspoon salt
        2 cups water
        1 tablespoon grated lemon rind
        3 tablespoons lemon juice
        ¼ cup butter

Mix together cornstarch, sugar, and salt in saucepan. Gradually stir in water. Cook, stirring constantly, until mixture boils and is thickened and clear. Remove from heat; stir in remaining ingredients. Serve warm over Molasses Cake. Makes 2¼ cups sauce.

Chiffon cakes use salad oil instead of butter, producing a very light, fine texture. Be sure to use oil of the finest quality with no taste of its own.

APPLESAUCE CHIFFON CAKE

> 2 cups sifted flour
> 1½ cups sugar
> 3 teaspoons baking powder
> 1 teaspoon salt
> ½ cup salad oil
> 8 eggs, separated
> ⅔ cup water
> 1 15-ounce jar applesauce (use 1 cup for cake, rest for glaze)
> ½ teaspoon cinnamon
> ½ teaspoon cream of tartar

Preheat oven to 325°F. Sift flour with sugar, baking powder, and salt into a mixing bowl. Make a well in the center and add oil, egg yolks, water, 1 cup applesauce, and cinnamon. Beat until batter is smooth. In another bowl, beat egg whites with cream of tartar until very stiff peaks form. Do not underbeat. Very carefully fold egg yolk mixture into egg whites, just until blended. Turn into an ungreased 10- by 4-inch tube pan. Bake for 55 minutes. Increase oven temperature to 350°F. Bake 10 minutes longer or until cake tester inserted in cake comes out clean. Invert pan and place tube over the neck of a bottle, so that cake is raised above table. Let cool completely. Loosen cake from sides of pan with a spatula. Ice with Applesauce Glaze. Serves 12 to 14.

> APPLESAUCE GLAZE:
> ½ cup applesauce (rest of 15-ounce jar)
> 1 tablespoon lemon juice
> 1 pound confectioners' sugar, sifted
> 1 egg white

Combine applesauce, lemon juice, and sugar. Beat egg white just until soft peaks form. Fold into applesauce mixture. Spoon or pour over cake, covering top and letting the rest run down the sides.

WALNUT-CHERRY CHIFFON CAKE

    2 cups sifted flour
 1½ cups sugar
    3 teaspoons baking powder
    1 teaspoon salt
  ⅔ cup cooking oil
    2 egg yolks
  ¼ cup syrup from maraschino cherries
  ½ cup water
    1 teaspoon vanilla
    1 tablespoon lemon juice
  ½ cup finely chopped maraschino cherries
  ⅔ cup walnuts, very finely chopped
       red food coloring, optional
    1 cup egg whites (7 or 8)
  ½ teaspoon cream of tartar
       Fluffy Icing

Resift flour with one cup sugar, baking powder, and salt into mixing bowl. Make a well in center and add oil, egg yolks, cherry juice, water, vanilla, and lemon juice. Beat to a smooth batter. Add chopped cherries and walnuts. Add red food coloring, if desired, to deepen pink color. In a large mixing bowl, beat egg whites with cream of tartar to soft peaks. Gradually beat in remaining ½ cup sugar to make stiff meringue. Do not underbeat. Pour batter slowly and gradually over beaten whites, while gently folding with a rubber scraper or large spoon. Fold in just until blended; do not stir. Pour into ungreased 10-inch tube pan. Bake at 325°F., below oven center, for 1 hour and 10 to 15 minutes. When baked, top surface of cake will spring back when lightly touched with fingers, and any "cracks" in top will look dry. Remove from oven and immediately turn pan upside down, placing the tube part over neck of funnel or bottle. Let hang until thoroughly cold. Loosen cake from sides and tube, turn pan over and hit edge sharply on table to loosen. Serve plain, with a light sifting of powdered sugar, or spread top and sides with Fluffy Icing. Makes one large cake, about 16 servings.

FLUFFY ICING:

1 *large egg white*
1 *cup granulated sugar*
¼ *teaspoon cream of tartar*
¼ *teaspoon salt*
3 *tablespoons maraschino cherry juice*
2 *tablespoons water*
  few drops red food coloring, optional
  walnut halves or large pieces

Measure egg white, sugar, cream of tartar, salt, cherry juice, and water in top of double boiler. Place over boiling water and beat steadily with rotary beater, 7 minutes, until icing holds its shape. Tint a delicate pink, if desired, with red food coloring. Cake may be decorated with walnut halves or large pieces. Makes icing for top and sides of one 10-inch tube cake.

CHOCOLATE APPLESAUCE CAKE

2 *squares unsweetened chocolate*
½ *cup butter or margarine*
1 *cup sugar*
½ *cup applesauce*
2 *eggs, well beaten*
1 *teaspoon vanilla*
1 *cup sifted flour*
½ *teaspoon baking soda*
½ *teaspoon salt*

Preheat oven to 350°F. Grease an 8-inch square pan and flour bottom. Melt chocolate and butter in a large, heavy saucepan over a very low heat, stirring constantly. Cool. Into same saucepan, add sugar, applesauce, eggs, and vanilla. Mix well. Sift dry ingredients together and add to pan; mix well. Pour batter into baking pan. Bake 50 to 60 minutes, until cake tester inserted in center comes out clean. Cool. Cut into 8 pieces and top each with Fluff Topping.

FLUFF TOPPING:

½ cup applesauce
2 cups (½ 9-ounce container) whipped topping

Fold applesauce into whipped topping. Makes 8 servings.

ORANGE SPONGE CAKE

1¼ cups sifted cake flour
¼ cup sugar
¼ teaspoon salt
1 teaspoon cream of tartar
5 eggs, separated
¼ cup sugar
¾ cup light corn syrup
1 teaspoon grated orange rind
1 teaspoon orange extract

Sift together flour, ¼ cup sugar, and salt three times. Add cream of tartar to egg whites and beat until slightly mounded when beater is raised; gradually beat in remaining ¼ cup sugar; slowly add corn syrup and continue beating until whites stand in firm peaks when beater is raised. Beat egg yolks and orange rind until thick and lemon colored. Beat in orange extract. Fold egg yolks into egg white mixture. Gradually fold in dry ingredients, sifting about ¼ cup at a time over surface. Turn into ungreased 10- by 4-inch tube pan. Cut through with spatula to remove large bubbles. Bake in 325°F. oven for 50 to 55 minutes or until cake is lightly browned. Invert pan and let cake stand about 1 hour or until cool. To remove from pan, loosen side with spatula. Frost with Fluffy Apricot Frosting if desired. Serves 12 to 14.

FLUFFY APRICOT FROSTING:

2 egg whites
⅔ cup light corn syrup
½ cup apricot preserves
few drops almond extract

Beat egg whites until stiff but not dry. Combine corn syrup and apricot preserves. Gradually beat into egg whites, continuing to beat until frosting forms firm peaks when beater is raised. Fold in almond extract. Makes enough to cover tops and sides of two 8-inch layers, one 9-inch square, or one 10-inch tube cake. To frost cake baked in one 1-quart ring mold, prepare half quantity.

TARTINE GENOISE

CAKE:

5 eggs
½ cup sugar
¾ cup sifted flour
5 ounces dark sweet chocolate (1 cup broken pieces)
¼ cup water

Beat eggs, gradually adding sugar, and beat with electric mixer 10 to 15 minutes at high speed. (Batter will be very thick.) Gradually blend in flour with wire whisk or scraper, cutting through slowly just to blend. Melt chocolate and water slowly over hot (not boiling) water, just to melt and blend. Gently fold in chocolate. Butter 9-inch spring form pan and fill with batter. Bake in 350°F. oven for 45 minutes or until cake shrinks from sides of pan. Remove from ring immediately to cool. Frost with Cocoa Chantilly. Makes 10 to 12 servings.

COCOA CHANTILLY:

1½ cups heavy cream
¼ cup cocoa
¼ cup sugar
mint extract, few drops
1 29-ounce can cling peach halves
sweet chocolate, grated

Combine heavy cream and cocoa; blend well and chill for 1 hour or longer before whipping (otherwise cream will not whip with the addition of cocoa). Whip until soft peaks form and flavor with sugar and 3 or 4 drops mint extract. Drain peach halves. Frost top of the cake with ⅔ of the whipped frosting and arrange peach halves on top. Use remaining frosting in pastry bag with star tip to decorate between peach halves and around edge of cake. Garnish peaches with grated chocolate. Keep cake chilled until ready to serve.

GÂTEAU SANS SOUCI

    1¼ cups sifted flour
     ¾ cup sugar
     ¼ cup corn starch
      2 teaspoons baking powder
     ½ teaspoon salt
     ½ cup corn oil
     ½ cup water
      2 eggs, separated
      2 teaspoons grated lemon rind
      1 29-ounce can cling peach slices
      1 17-ounce can apricot halves
    1½ cups fresh strawberries
      6 tablespoons Cointreau liqueur
    1½ pints heavy cream
      3 tablespoons sugar

Grease two 8-inch layer cake pans and line bottoms with waxed paper. Sift flour, sugar, corn starch, baking powder and salt together into a mixing bowl. Combine corn oil, water, egg yolks, and grated lemon rind. Add to dry ingredients and beat until smooth. Beat egg whites until peaks form. Fold into batter. Pour into prepared pans. Bake in a 400°F. oven until lightly browned and firm, about 25 to 30 minutes. Cool and then chill in refrigerator before putting the cake together. Drain peach slices and apricots. Rinse and drain strawberries and remove hulls. Sprinkle each fruit with 2 tablespoons Cointreau liqueur. Cut chilled cake layers crosswise, making four layers. Beat cream until stiff and flavor with sugar. Put layers together with whipped cream and fruit, using a different fruit for each layer, reserving ⅓ cup of each fruit for garnish. To obtain classic effect, use pastry bag with star tip filled with remaining whipped cream, and make swirls and stars on sides of cake. Keep cake chilled until ready to serve. Makes 10 to 12 servings.

PINEAPPLE CHIFFON CHEESECAKE
WITH CHERRY TOPPING

CRUST:
1½ cups graham cracker crumbs
¼ cup sugar
½ cup butter, melted

In a bowl combine crumbs and sugar; stir in butter. Press mixture firmly and evenly against the bottom and side of a 9-inch spring form pan. Chill.

CHEESECAKE:
2 envelopes (2 tablespoons) unflavored gelatin
½ cup cold water
½ cup sugar
2 teaspoons cornstarch
½ cup milk
2 egg yolks, beaten
2 cups cottage cheese, sieved
1 8¾-ounce can crushed pineapple in heavy syrup
1 tablespoon lemon rind
3 tablespoons fresh lemon juice
2 egg whites
1 cup heavy cream

Soften gelatin in water. In a 1-quart saucepan mix ¼ cup sugar and cornstarch. Gradually add milk. Cook over medium heat, stirring constantly, until mixture thickens. Add small amount of hot mixture to egg yolks; return all to saucepan. Cook 1 additional minute. Add softened gelatin; stir until dissolved. Pour into bowl; cool to lukewarm. Add cottage cheese, pineapple with syrup, lemon rind and juice to gelatin mixture. In a small mixing bowl beat egg whites until foamy; continue beating; gradually add remaining ¼ cup sugar and beat until stiff peaks form. Fold beaten egg whites into cheese mixture. Whip cream until stiff; fold into mixture. Pour into crust; chill until set.

CHERRY TOPPING:
  2 cups (21-ounce can) cherry pie filling
  1 tablespoon butter
  ½ teaspoon almond extract

In a 1-quart saucepan cook cherry pie filling over medium heat, stirring occasionally, for about 5 minutes. Stir in butter to melt. Add almond extract. Chill sauce; spoon over cheesecake. Chill several hours before serving. Makes 10 to 12 servings.

PINEAPPLE CHIFFON CHEESECAKE WITH CHERRY TOPPING

ORANGE CHEESECAKE

CRUST:
1 *cup sifted flour*
¼ *cup sugar*
1 *tablespoon grated orange rind*
½ *cup butter*
1 *egg yolk*
½ *teaspoon vanilla*

Combine flour, sugar, and grated orange rind. Cut in butter until mixture resembles coarse meal. Add egg yolk and vanilla; blend well. Pat ⅓ of the dough on bottom of a 9-inch spring form pan. Bake in a 400°F. oven 5 minutes or until golden brown. Cool. Pat remaining dough evenly around sides of pan to ½ inch from top.

ORANGE CHEESE FILLING:
5 *8-ounce packages cream cheese, at room temperature*
1¾ *cups sugar*
3 *tablespoons flour*
1 *tablespoon grated orange rind*
¼ *teaspoon salt*
¼ *teaspoon vanilla*
5 *eggs*
2 *egg yolks*
¼ *cup frozen orange juice concentrate, thawed, undiluted*
   orange sections
   mint sprigs

Combine cheese, sugar, flour, orange rind, salt, and vanilla in large bowl of electric mixer. Beat at low speed until smooth. Beat in eggs and egg yolks, one at a time, beating well after each addition. Stir in undiluted orange concentrate. Pour into prepared pan. Place aluminum foil under pan on oven rack and bake in 400°F. oven 8 to 10 minutes, until crust browns lightly. Reduce heat to 225°F. and bake 1 hour and 20 minutes longer. Turn oven off and leave cake inside to cool for one hour, or cool slowly (do not put in very cold place) and then refrigerate. Serve garnished with orange sections and mint sprigs. Makes 12 to 18 servings.

If you like your cheesecake firm and creamy smooth, you'll love this one. I often bake it in a spring form without the cookie crust, and find that it holds its shape beautifully. Either way, it's very special.

STRAWBERRY CHEESECAKE

COOKIE CRUST:
1 cup sifted flour
¼ cup sugar
1 teaspoon grated lemon rind
½ cup butter
1 egg yolk

Combine flour and sugar; add grated lemon rind. With your hands or a dough hook of an electric mixer, work in butter and egg yolk. Mix until a soft dough is formed. Place in a 10-inch spring form pan and press over bottom and sides, completely covering the interior of the pan. Bake in a 350°F. oven for 10 minutes, or until very lightly browned. Cool.

FILLING:
6 eggs, separated
1 pound cream cheese, softened to room temperature
1 pint dairy sour cream
1 cup sugar
3 tablespoons flour
2 teaspoons lemon juice

Beat egg yolks until thick and lemon colored. Mash cream cheese until soft, and add to egg yolks; beat thoroughly. Add sour cream. Add sugar, flour, and lemon juice. Beat egg whites until stiff peaks form; fold through the cream cheese batter until completely combined. Pour into the prepared cookie crust. Bake at 300°F. for 1 hour; then turn oven off and let cake come to room temperature for at least 1 hour before removing from the oven. When the cake is completely cooled, refrigerate. Several hours before serving, top with Strawberry Topping. Makes 12 servings.

STRAWBERRY TOPPING:
1 *quart fresh strawberries*
¾ *cup sugar*
¼ *cup cold water*
1 *teaspoon lemon juice*
1½ *tablespoons cornstarch*
1 *teaspoon butter*
several drops of red food coloring

Wash and hull berries, setting aside enough berries to crush and make 1 cupful. Arrange remaining berries in concentric circles on the top of the cake. Place crushed berries, sugar, water, lemon juice, and cornstarch in a saucepan. Heat and stir until berries cook and sugar dissolves; and as mixture thickens stir in butter and red food coloring. Cook for several minutes, stirring constantly, until mixture gets very thick and suddenly becomes clear. Remove from heat, cool slightly, and spoon carefully over berries on top of cheesecake. Cover berries and spaces between with this glaze. Then refrigerate again, until ready to serve. To serve, remove sides of spring form, and let bottom remain to support the cake.

APPLESAUCE MANDARIN CHEESECAKE

CRUST:
1½ *cups graham cracker crumbs*
¼ *cup butter, melted*
45 *chocolate-covered sugar wafer sticks*

Mix graham cracker crumbs with butter. Pour mixture into a 9-inch spring form pan. Press evenly into bottom of pan. Stand chocolate sticks around edge of pan.

FILLING:
3 *envelopes (3 tablespoons) unflavored gelatin*
1 *cup orange juice*
2 *8-ounce packages cream cheese, at room temperature*
⅓ *cup sugar*

APPLESAUCE MANDARIN CHEESECAKE

2 cups canned applesauce
   grated rind and juice of 1 lemon
2 cups heavy cream, whipped
2 11-ounce cans mandarin oranges, drained

Sprinkle gelatin in orange juice. Let stand 5 minutes. Put over low heat and stir until gelatin is dissolved. Gradually beat orange juice into cream cheese. Fold in sugar, applesauce, lemon rind and juice, and 3 cups of the whipped cream. Fold in 1½ cans of mandarin oranges.

Pour mixture into chocolate-stick-lined spring form pan. Chill until firm. Unmold cake. Use remaining whipped cream as garnish for cake and decorate with remaining orange sections. Makes 10 to 12 servings.

Pashka is an elegant cheesecake that originates from Russia. There it is molded in special triangular molds, but Russian-Americans use a flowerpot lined with layers of cheesecloth and weighted with something heavy. The trick is to drain most of the liquid from the cheese, leaving a smooth and compact creamy mixture. Pashka is generally served with a sweet coffee cake or baba.

PASHKA

1 *pound soft unsalted butter*
2 *cups sugar*
3 *pounds pot cheese*
3 *egg yolks*
1 *6-ounce can frozen orange juice concentrate, thawed, undiluted*
1 *4½-ounce can whole blanched almonds, ground*
   orange slices
   citron or angelica

Cream butter with sugar in large bowl of electric mixer. Gradually beat in pot cheese and continue beating until very smooth and creamy. Beat in egg yolks, undiluted orange juice concentrate, and ground almonds. Line a 7-inch flowerpot (one with a hole in the bottom, and that will hold 8 cups) with several layers of cheesecloth. Turn cheese mixture into pot and pack tightly. Cover with cheesecloth, place in a shallow pan, and put weights or something heavy on top. (If necessary, put a small plate on top of cheese mixture before adding weights, to distribute the weight evenly.) Refrigerate for at least 24 hours, pouring off the liquid that drains from the flowerpot every few hours. To serve, turn cheese mixture out of flowerpot and remove cheesecloth. Garnish with orange slices and pieces of citron or angelica. Makes 16 servings.

DARK CHERRY DIET CHEESECAKE
(A Diet Dessert)

DIET CHEESECAKE:

1 *cup skim milk*

4 *eggs*

2 *envelopes (2 tablespoons) unflavored gelatin*

1 *cup sugar*

1 *teaspoon vanilla*

2 *pounds cream-style cottage cheese, sieved or blended*

Pour milk into top of double boiler. Beat in eggs until well combined. Mix gelatin and sugar, stir into milk-egg mixture. Cook over boiling water, stirring constantly, until gelatin is dissolved and mixture has thickened, 10 to 15 minutes. Remove from heat and cool slightly. Stir vanilla into sieved cottage cheese; mix well. Stir in custard mixture; mix well. Pour into 8-inch spring form pan. Chill until almost firm. Cover with Dark Sweet Cherry Topping. Chill at least 1 hour longer. At serving time, remove side of pan and place cheesecake on serving platter. Makes about 10 servings.

DARK SWEET CHERRY TOPPING:

1 *14½-ounce jar pitted dark sweet cherries*

1 *teaspoon cornstarch*

Drain syrup from jar of dark sweet cherries into a saucepan. Stir in cornstarch. Bring to boil, stirring constantly. Cook 1 minute longer. Arrange drained cherries on top of cheesecake. Spoon ¼ to ⅓ cup thickened syrup over cherries. Chill. Rest of syrup may be spooned over portions of cheesecake at serving time, if desired.

10

Exquisite Tortes

When you think of the word TORTE, *think of several layers of richness, usually comprised of ground nut batter and whipped cream or sweet icing. Sometimes a thin layer of jam or fruit is also included. The elaborateness is reflected not only in the ingredients, but also in the many steps involved in its creation. It is truly the toothsome wonder of the baking world.*

The tortes of Scandinavia, Germany, Austria, and France have a many-layered, cakelike appearance, while those of Italy are a dieter's daydream of whipped cream, suspended at times with layers of light meringue or surrounded with cream puffs on a thinly baked base.

The shape is always round, no matter how many layers are used or how many pans needed, and the taste should always be an incredible experience.

CHOCOLATE-APRICOT WHIPPED CREAM TORTE

CHOCOLATE-APRICOT WHIPPED CREAM TORTE

⅓ cup butter
1 cup sugar
½ teaspoon salt
5 egg yolks
1 whole egg
3 squares unsweetened chocolate, melted
¾ cup ground almonds
5 egg whites
1½ cups heavy cream
1 cup apricot jam

Cream butter with sugar and salt until light and fluffy. Stir in egg yolks and whole egg; cream well. Thoroughly beat in melted chocolate. Stir in almonds. Beat egg whites until mixture will form stiff, shiny peaks. Fold carefully into the chocolate mixture. Pour into three 8-inch layer cake pans which have been lined on bottoms with wax paper. Bake at 350°F. for 15 to 20 minutes. Cool for 15 minutes; then remove from pans and cool thoroughly on racks. Whip cream just until soft peaks will form. Stir jam to break up; then fold into whipped cream. Spread between layers and over top of torte. If desired, garnish with additional whipped cream. Chill at least 2 hours. Makes about 16 servings.

When in Vienna, I set out to do a cook's taste tour of Sacher Torte as served at the Hotel Sacher, Demel's, and every other fine restaurant in town. Each variation of this world-famous torte was incredibly delicious. While the argument goes on about who has the original secret recipe, many Austrian housewives have heirloom recipes for the same chocolate delight. Here is such a version for Sacher Torte. Serve it with a mound of whipped cream if you wish to do as the Viennese do.

SACHER TORTE

>   1 *cup semisweet chocolate morsels*
>   1 *tablespoon rum*
>   ⅔ *cup butter*
>   1 *cup confectioners' sugar*
>   6 *eggs, separated*
>   1 *cup flour, sifted*
>   ½ *cup apricot jam*
>   1 *cup semisweet chocolate morsels*
>   2 *tablespoons water*

Melt 1 cup chocolate morsels in the top half of a double boiler over simmering water; stir in rum. Remove from heat and cool slightly. Cream butter; add sugar and again cream well. Add egg yolks one at a time. Add melted chocolate mixture and stir well. Beat egg whites until stiff. Fold egg whites into the chocolate mixture, alternately with the flour. Pour into a greased and floured 9-inch layer cake pan and bake in a 325°F. oven for about 50 minutes. Remove from oven and cool. To frost, remove from pan; warm apricot jam and spread on top and sides. Melt chocolate morsels, using the same method as above, and adding water to thin. Spread over top and sides of cake. Makes 10 to 12 servings.

CHOCOLATE TORTE

CAKE:
⅔ cup margarine
1 cup sugar
6 eggs, separated
4 ounces unsweetened chocolate, melted
½ cup finely grated almonds
1 cup sifted flour
¼ cup sugar

Grease and flour one 9-inch spring form pan. Blend margarine with 1 cup sugar. Beat egg yolks until thick and lemon colored, then stir into margarine-sugar mixture. Blend in melted chocolate and grated almonds. Fold in flour. Beat egg whites until frothy, then gradually add ¼ cup sugar, beating until soft peaks form when beater is raised. Fold into chocolate mixture. Pour batter into prepared pan. Bake in 300°F. oven 50 to 60 minutes or until cake springs back when touched lightly with finger. Cool overnight, then remove from pan. Split cake into two layers. Fill and frost.

FILLING AND FROSTING:
1¼ cups apricot preserves
⅓ cup light corn syrup
3 ounces unsweetened chocolate
2 teaspoons hot water
chopped pistachio nuts, optional

Spread about ½ cup apricot preserves on top of one layer; stack second layer on top. Spread remaining preserves over top and sides of torte. Bring light corn syrup to boil in small saucepan. Remove from heat and add unsweetened chocolate. Let stand until chocolate is melted and syrup is cooled to lukewarm. Blend chocolate and syrup, then stir in hot water. Quickly spread on top and sides of torte. Garnish sides with chopped pistachio nuts. Makes 10 to 12 servings.

CHOCOLATE CHIP TORTE

Here's another one-layer torte that is easy to bake and delicious too. You can grind nuts easily with an electric blender, or purchase them already ground in a can. This cake may also be baked in a 10-inch tube pan—remember to grease and crumb the bottom only, giving the spongy batter an opportunity to climb up the sides of the pan.

CHOCOLATE CHIP TORTE

½ cup butter
1 cup sugar
5 eggs, separated
½ cup sifted flour
1 teaspoon baking powder
½ teaspoon salt
1 cup ground almonds
6 squares semisweet chocolate, grated
   bread crumbs
   confectioners' sugar
   whipped cream, optional

Cream butter. Gradually blend in sugar, creaming well after each addition. Slightly beat egg yolks; add to butter and beat well. Sift flour with baking powder and salt. Add ground almonds; add to egg yolk mixture. Beat egg whites until stiff peaks form; fold into flour mixture. Fold in grated chocolate. Grease and sprinkle with bread crumbs the bottom of a 9-inch spring form pan. Pour mixture into pan. Bake at 350°F. for 50 to 60 minutes, or until cake springs back when lightly pressed with finger. Cool in pan for 10 minutes; then remove side from pan (if using a spring form, otherwise, remove cake from tube pan) and finish cooling. Sift confectioners' sugar over top. Serve with whipped cream, if desired. Makes 10 to 12 servings.

*Black Forest Torte sometimes has a layer of cherries in the
middle layer. If you want to try it that way, spread drained
canned sweet pitted cherries over the frosting on the second
layer.*

BLACK FOREST TORTE

    1¾ cups unsifted flour
    1¾ cups sugar
    1¼ teaspoons baking soda
     ½ teaspoon salt
     ¼ teaspoon double-acting baking powder
     ⅔ cup soft-type margarine
      4 squares unsweetened chocolate, melted and cooled
    1¼ cups water
      1 teaspoon vanilla
      3 eggs
      2 4-ounce packages sweet cooking chocolate
     ¾ cup soft-type margarine
     ½ cup chopped toasted almonds
      2 cups heavy cream
      1 tablespoon sugar
      1 teaspoon vanilla

In large bowl of mixer, combine flour, 1¾ cups of sugar, the soda, salt,
baking powder, ⅔ cup margarine, melted unsweetened chocolate, water,
and 1 teaspoon vanilla. Beat at low speed to blend; then beat 2 minutes
at medium speed, scraping sides and bottom of bowl frequently. Add eggs;
beat 2 minutes longer. Pour batter into four 9-inch layer cake pans which
have been lined with wax paper. Layers will be thin. Bake at 350°F. for
17 to 20 minutes, or until cake tester inserted into center comes out clean.
Cool slightly in pans; then remove from pans and finish cooling on racks.
Melt 1½ packages of sweet cooking chocolate over hot water. Cool.
Blend in ¾ cup margarine and the almonds. Whip the cream with 1
tablespoon sugar and 1 teaspoon vanilla. Do not overbeat. Place 1 layer
of cake on serving plate; spread with half the sweet chocolate mixture;
top with next layer and spread with half of the whipped cream. Repeat
layers, ending with whipped cream on top. Do not frost sides. Using a

vegetable peeler, make chocolate curls from remaining half package of sweet cooking chocolate, using to decorate top completely. Cover with transparent plastic wrap. Refrigerate until ready to serve. Serves 16.

TEN-LAYER CHOCOLATE-ICED TORTE

LAYERS:

2 cups sugar

¾ cup butter

6 eggs, separated

½ cup milk

2 cups flour

1 teaspoon baking powder

½ teaspoon baking soda

Cream sugar and butter well. Add slightly beaten egg yolks. Add milk. Sift flour, baking powder, and baking soda together; add to batter in small quantities, beating well after each addition. Beat egg whites until stiff; fold into batter. Spoon batter into a greased 9-inch layer cake pan, until just the bottom of the pan is covered. Bake in a 400°F. oven for 10 minutes, or until lightly browned. Remove from pan onto rack and cool. Repeat the process until you have baked ten layers.

CHOCOLATE ICING:

1¾ cups milk

1¾ cups sugar

8 ounces bitter chocolate

1 teaspoon vanilla

1 tablespoon vanilla

Cook the milk, sugar, and chocolate together in the top of a double boiler over hot water, stirring frequently. When chocolate is melted and the mixture is thickened, add the vanilla and butter. Mix thoroughly. Cool. Spread between the cake layers and over the top, but not around the sides. Makes 12 servings.

It is as much fun for me to visit the kitchens of a de luxe hotel as it is for someone else to go to a ball game. For techniques and products differ from country to country, as is visible in the great kitchens.

The time I spent with Chef Friedrich Dekan at the Imperial Hotel in Vienna was fascinating, and I bring you as a souvenir—the famous Imperial Torte. Hotels and restaurants in Europe buy marzipan ready-made from one of the few factories that specialize in grinding the sweet and bitter almonds together in just the right way. Scandinavian and Austrian chefs are fond of using marzipan for smooth tops and decorated sides of their gorgeous cake creations. Fortunately, you can buy marzipan in gourmet food stores, but if you can't find it, just grind up an equal amount of almonds and confectioners' sugar, and bind it together with a beaten egg white until you get the consistency of a soft dough. Then roll it out as you would a pie crust. Just don't let it stop you from trying this fabulous Imperial Torte.

IMPERIAL TORTE

LAYERS:
  2 egg whites
1¼ cups sugar
  2 cups ground almonds

Beat egg whites until almost stiff; gradually add sugar and beat until very stiff. Mix in almonds. Spread a thin layer in the bottom of five greased 9-inch layer cake pans (or line cookie sheets with greased aluminum foil and draw 9-inch circles, then cover with a thin layer of batter) and bake in a 225°F. oven for 40 minutes, or until lightly browned. Remove from pans carefully and cool. Then spread with Chocolate Crème between layers, and follow directions for Icing. Makes 10 to 12 servings.

CHOCOLATE CRÈME:
½ cup butter
4 egg yolks

    4 *ounces baking chocolate*
    4 *ounces unsweetened cocoa*
    1 *tablespoon ground almonds*
    1 *tablespoon cognac*

Cream butter; add egg yolks. Melt chocolate in the top of a double boiler over simmering water; stir in cocoa and mix until smooth. Stir chocolate mixture into butter mixture. Add nuts and cognac. Beat very well. Spread thin between cooled layers. Then follow directions for Icing.

ICING:
    1 *8-ounce package marzipan (almond-sugar mixture available in gourmet food stores)*
    1 *tablespoon apricot jam*
    1 *cup sugar*
    ¼ *cup water*
    1 *teaspoon light corn syrup*
    1 *tablespoon strong coffee*

With a rolling pin, shape the marzipan into a 9-inch circle to fit the top of the torte layers. Place it on top, lightly pressing edges so it will adhere. Warm apricot jam and brush over the marzipan in a very thin layer. Combine sugar and water in a saucepan; stir to dissolve, and then add corn syrup. Boil quickly and then remove from heat. Sprinkle top of mixture with cold water, and stir with a spatula until a fine, smooth white paste is formed. Work in cold coffee until smooth. Warm gently until it is spreadable, and spread over top of torte.

LIME-PINEAPPLE TORTE

CRUST:
1 cup sifted flour
¼ cup sugar
½ cup butter
½ cup finely chopped nuts

In a bowl combine flour and sugar. With a pastry blender or two knives, cut in butter until mixture resembles cornmeal. Stir in nuts. Press in bottom of shallow baking pan, 13 by 9 by 2 inches. Bake in a preheated 400°F. oven for 15 minutes. Cool on wire rack. Meanwhile, prepare filling.

FILLING:
1 20½-ounce can crushed pineapple
1 cup pineapple syrup
1 3-ounce package lime flavor gelatin
1 8-ounce package cream cheese
¾ cup sugar
⅛ teaspoon peppermint extract
⅔ cup whipping cream

Drain pineapple; reserve 1 cup syrup. In a saucepan heat syrup to boiling. In a bowl pour pineapple syrup over gelatin; stir to dissolve; cool slightly. In a small mixing bowl beat together cream cheese and sugar until light and fluffy. Gradually add gelatin mixture and beat until blended. Stir in pineapple and the peppermint extract; chill until partially set. In a mixing bowl whip cream until stiff; fold into gelatin mixture. Pour mixture over baked crust. Chill. Immediately prepare glaze.

GLAZE:
½ cup semisweet chocolate pieces
1 tablespoon butter
⅓ cup whipping cream
¼ teaspoon peppermint extract

In a saucepan over low heat combine chocolate pieces, butter, and whipping cream. Heat over low heat, stirring constantly until smooth. Stir in peppermint extract. Drizzle chocolate sauce over top of partially set dessert. Chill at least 4 hours. Cut in squares to serve. Makes 20 servings.

LINZER TORTE

    1 *cup butter*
    ¾ *cup granulated sugar*
    3 *egg yolks*
        grated rind of 1 lemon
 1½ *cups sifted flour*
    1 *cup ground walnuts*
    1 *teaspoon cinnamon*
    1 *cup thick raspberry jam*
    1 *egg*
    1 *tablespoon cream*
   ¼ *cup confectioners' sugar*

Cream butter until light; slowly beat in granulated sugar and continue beating until light and fluffy. Beat in egg yolks and lemon rind. Blend in flour, walnuts, and cinnamon. Shape dough into a ball and chill for a minimum of 1 hour or as long as 12 hours. Work with about three-quarters of dough; set rest aside. Roll, or push dough out, with fingers, to fit bottom and up the sides of a lightly greased 9-inch round layer cake pan. Dough should be between ¼ and ½ inch thick all around. Spread with jam. Roll out remaining dough and cut strips about ½ inch wide. Lay these in lattice fashion across jam leaving ½ inch between each strip. Roll top edge of dough down from sides of pan and pinch over ends of these strips to secure them. Beat egg and cream; brush all over exposed dough. Chill for half hour. Bake at 350°F. about 45 minutes. Cool; sift confectioners' sugar over top. When cold, the Torte may be gently inverted onto a cooling rack and then turned back onto a serving plate. Makes about 10 servings.

APRICOT-ALMOND TORTE

> 1   recipe Torte Shell (below)
> ⅓ cup apricot preserves
> 1⅓ cups sifted cake flour
> ⅔ cup sugar
> 1½ teaspoons baking powder
> ½ teaspoon salt
> ½ cup finely chopped lightly toasted blanched almonds
> ⅓ cup corn oil
> 2   eggs, separated
> ½ cup milk
> 1   teaspoon almond extract
> ⅛ teaspoon cream of tartar
> ¼ cup apricot preserves
>   Apricot Frosting

Prepare Torte Shell as directed; brush entire surface with ⅓ cup apricot preserves. Sift together cake flour, sugar, baking powder, and salt. Stir in almonds. Make well in center; add corn oil, egg yolks, milk, and almond extract; beat until smooth. Beat egg whites and cream of tartar until very stiff peaks form when beater is raised. Gently fold into flour mixture until well blended. Turn into Torte Shell. Bake in 350°F. oven 40 to 45 minutes or until cake springs back when touched. Cool about 10 minutes on cake rack or until pastry shrinks from pan. Remove from pan. Cool completely. Spread top of cake with ¼ cup apricot preserves. Using a pastry bag, decorate top of cake with rosettes of Apricot Frosting. Makes 8 to 10 servings.

> TORTE SHELL:
> 1½ cups sifted flour
> 2   tablespoons sugar
> ¼ teaspoon salt
> ½ cup margarine
> 1   egg, separated (reserve egg white for Apricot Frosting)

Sift together flour, sugar, and salt into mixing bowl. Cut in margarine with pastry blender or 2 knives until well mixed and coarse crumbs form. Mix in egg yolk. Knead until smooth dough forms. Press evenly and firmly against bottom and sides of 9- by 1½-inch layer cake pan. Set aside while preparing cake.

APRICOT FROSTING:

1 egg white (from Torte Shell)
⅓ cup apricot preserves
1 tablespoon sugar
¼ teaspoon almond extract

Beat together egg white and apricot preserves until soft peaks form when beater is raised. Gradually add sugar, beating until very stiff peaks form. Mix in almond extract. Makes 1 cup.

NUT TORTE

3 tablespoons margarine
2 tablespoons cornstarch
2½ cups milk
3 egg yolks, slightly beaten
2 cups walnuts, grated
1 teaspoon grated lemon rind
⅛ teaspoon cinnamon
3 egg whites
½ cup sugar
1 recipe pastry for double-crust pie (page 119)

Melt margarine in top of double boiler. Remove from heat. Blend in cornstarch, then milk. Stirring constantly, bring to boil over medium heat and boil 1 minute. Stir a small amount of hot mixture into egg yolks, then stir all into remaining mixture in double boiler top. Cook over boiling water, stirring occasionally, until mixture thickens slightly, about 2 minutes. Combine nuts, lemon rind, and cinnamon; stir into hot pudding. Beat egg whites until foamy; gradually add sugar, beating until soft peaks form when beater is raised. Fold into pudding.

Roll out pastry and line one 15½- by 10½- by 1-inch jelly roll pan. Spread pudding mixture over pastry. Bake in 425°F. oven until golden brown, about 30 minutes. Serve warm or cool, topped with whipped cream. Serves 8 to 10.

As you may already have learned, some of the best food of Italy can be found in the local trattorias. Such a place is the Trattoria Cammillo in Florence, where Masiero Bruno presides with well-earn pride. Here diners can enjoy generous portions of his Saint-Honoré Torte. It requires many steps in a home kitchen, but is not as difficult as it is time consuming— so save it for one of those creative days.

SAINT-HONORÉ TORTE

TORTE BASE:

2 cups flour
¼ cup sugar
1 cup butter, at room temperature
2 egg yolks
1 teaspoon vanilla

Place flour on a pastry board and make a deep well in the center. Mix the sugar, butter, and egg yolks in this well; add the vanilla. Then carefully work the surrounding flour into the mixture. Refrigerate the dough for an hour. Then roll it out thick (or pat it evenly) to fit the bottom of a 10-inch spring form. Bake at 350°F. for about 20 minutes, or until lightly browned. Remove from oven and cool.

Meanwhile, prepare Small Cream Puffs and Filling.

SMALL CREAM PUFFS:

½ cup butter
1 cup water
1 cup flour
  dash of salt
3 eggs

Put butter and water in a saucepan and cook until butter is melted. Stir in flour and salt, mixing briskly until it no longer sticks to the sides of the saucepan. Remove from heat and beat in one egg at a time. Drop a heaping rounded teaspoonful of the mixture every two inches, on a well-greased cookie sheet. Shape the dough into a round ball with the back of the spoon if it seems to need it. Then bake in a 375°F. oven for about 40 minutes. Remove from oven and cool on a rack. Slit sides of puffs and fill with the following cream:

CREAM FILLING FOR PUFFS:
½ cup sugar
1 tablespoon cornstarch
1 cup scalded light cream
2 egg yolks, slightly beaten
½ teaspoon vanilla

Mix the sugar and cornstarch together; pour in the scalded cream and then stir the entire mixture into the slightly beaten egg yolks. Add vanilla. Cook this in the top of a double boiler over simmering water, stirring constantly until mixture thickens. Cool and use as filling for cream puffs. Then assemble Torte.

TO ASSEMBLE TORTE:
Torte base
¼ cup confectioners' sugar
2 tablespoons hot water
filled Cream Puffs
2 cups heavy cream
¼ cup confectioners' sugar
1 teaspoon vanilla
1 cup sweet chocolate shavings

Remove side of spring form. Stir ¼ cup confectioners' sugar and hot water together to form a thin icing; use this to stick the cream puffs all around the edge of the torte base. (Use extra icing for tops of extra cream puffs and refrigerate to serve another time.) Be sure that the cream puffs are set close together, touching each other and forming a framework for the whipped cream filling. Place heavy cream in a chilled bowl and beat; add ¼ cup confectioners' sugar and vanilla while the cream is beating. When it reaches the thickened whipped stage, stop at once (otherwise you are on to making butter). Fill prepared torte base with the whipped cream. Top with chocolate shavings. Chill until serving time. Makes 12 servings.

BUTTERSCOTCH-NUT TORTE

TORTE:
  6 eggs, separated
  ½ cup sugar
  1 teaspoon baking powder
  2 teaspoons vanilla
  1 teaspoon almond extract
  1 cup sugar
  2 cups graham cracker crumbs
  1 cup finely chopped walnuts
  1 cup heavy cream, whipped and sweetened
      walnut halves for garnish

Separate eggs. Beat egg yolks until thick and lemon colored. Beat in gradually ½ cup sugar, baking powder, vanilla, and almond extracts. Beat egg whites until soft peaks form; add the remaining 1 cup sugar, a tablespoon at a time, and continue beating until stiff. Gently fold in the yolks, cracker crumbs, and nuts. Pour into a lined but ungreased 9-inch spring form pan. Bake in a 325°F. oven for one hour. Remove from oven and cool in pan on a rack for 10 minutes. Remove carefully from pan and place on serving dish; gently peel off paper. Cool until ready to serve. Just before serving, frost top of Torte only with whipped cream. Serve with Butterscotch Sauce.

BUTTERSCOTCH SAUCE:
  1 cup brown sugar
  1 tablespoon flour
  ¼ cup orange juice
  ¼ cup water
  ¼ cup butter
  2 eggs, beaten
  ½ teaspoon vanilla

Combine sugar and flour in small saucepan. Blend in orange juice, water, and butter. Cook over low heat, stirring constantly, until thickened. Slowly add a small amount of hot mixture to eggs, stirring constantly; return to saucepan and cook one minute longer. Remove from heat; add vanilla. Cool the sauce before serving. Cut Torte and pour Sauce over individual pieces. Makes 6 to 8 servings.

WALNUT AMBROSIA TORTE

>   6 *eggs*
>   1 *cup granulated sugar*
>   ⅛ *teaspoon salt*
>   1 *teaspoon brandy flavoring*
>   1 *cup sifted cake flour*
>   1 *cup ground walnuts*
>   1 *tablespoon finely grated orange rind*
>   2 *tablespoons melted butter*
>   1 *pint heavy cream*
>   ⅓ *cup sugar*
>   2 *teaspoons brandy flavoring*
>   1 *cup drained, diced, fresh or canned peaches*
>   1 *pint basket fresh strawberries or 1 10-ounce package frozen*
>   *strawberries*

In a large bowl beat eggs until thick and lemon colored. Slowly add 1 cup sugar, continuing to beat; allow a total of 10 minutes beating time. Add salt and 1 teaspoon brandy flavoring. Sift cake flour over batter; sprinkle walnuts and orange rind over flour; fold in until well blended. Fold in melted butter. Pour into two greased and floured 9-inch round layer cake pans. Bake at 350°F. about 30 minutes until cake tests done. Remove from pans to cool. When cold split layers with sharp knife. Whip cream; beat in ⅓ cup sugar and 2 teaspoons brandy flavoring; divide into two equal portions. Add peaches to one portion and use this as a filling to reassemble cake layers. Frost with remaining cream and decorate with halved fresh berries, or crush frozen berries and serve as a sauce with the torte. Makes 10 to 12 servings.

From Florence, Italy, comes this Cavour Torte, so typical of all the beautiful dessert efforts of that historic city of art. The three layers are of melt-in-your-mouth meringue, slathered with strawberries and whipped cream in between. Fantastic!

CAVOUR TORTE

    10 egg whites
    3⅜ cups sugar
    1½ teaspoons vanilla
     2 cups heavy cream, whipped
     1 pint fresh strawberries, halved

Beat egg whites until stiff peaks form; then beat in sugar by adding gradually. Beat in vanilla. Grease three 9-inch layer cake pans; spread egg white mixture over bottoms of each. Bake 1 hour in a 275°F. oven, or longer until lightly browned and crisp. Carefully remove meringues from pans. Mix the whipped cream and strawberries together. Spread the first meringue with half the whipped cream and strawberries. Top with second meringue. Repeat with remaining whipped cream mixture; top with third meringue. Chill. Makes 8 to 10 servings.

ROMAN TORTE

    CAKE:
     3 eggs
    ½ cup sugar
    ¼ teaspoon salt
    ½ cup sifted flour
     6 tablespoons cornstarch

Beat eggs in small mixer bowl until fluffy. Gradually add sugar and salt, beating until mixture is doubled in bulk and mounds slightly when dropped from spoon. Sift flour and cornstarch over egg mixture; fold in. Pour into greased 9-inch spring form pan. Bake in 350°F. oven until top springs back when lightly touched, 30 to 35 minutes. Cool slightly. Remove from pan. Cool completely. Slice crosswise into 3 layers.

FILLING AND TOPPING:

¾ cup margarine
1 cup confectioners' sugar
4 egg yolks
1 cup chocolate syrup
2 tablespoons instant coffee powder
   Cointreau, brandy, or other liqueur
½ pint heavy cream

Blend margarine and sugar. Add egg yolks one at a time, blending well. Mix in chocolate syrup and coffee powder. Line bottom and sides of a 9-inch spring form pan or deep-sided pan with plastic film. Place 1 cake layer in bottom of pan. Sprinkle with liqueur. Top with half the chocolate mixture. Repeat. Top with remaining cake layer and more liqueur. Cover with plastic film, then with plate or lid that fits just inside pan. Weight with heavy object. Refrigerate overnight. Just before serving, whip cream, and sweeten if desired. Invert cake on serving plate and frost top and sides with whipped cream. Makes 12 to 15 servings.

11

Dainty Tartlets, Cookies, and Small Cakes

There are times when you may prefer to serve individually baked desserts or a selection of pickup cookies, without losing the quality of a charming offering. As you will see from the recipes in this chapter, it is possible to meet both goals with considerable success.

Tartlet pans range from tiny shaped bite-size to small individual pie-size tins. If you cannot find them in your local kitchenware store, try the nearest restaurant supply store, or a shop specializing in gourmet utensils.

You will find the individual meringues to be especially delightful with their flavored custard fillings and melt-in-your-mouth crusts. The meringues themselves may be made ahead and frozen if necessary, thawing just before filling, for best results.

Notice also that the cookies all have a special flair, and would attract more attention if several kinds are served at once. Because of their size, the serving platter is of great importance if you want to achieve well-deserved approval of your baking efforts. Do choose one that will do these cookies justice. Pass them around with a portion of fruit compote or sherbet if you desire.

STRAWBERRY TARTLETS

> 1 *pint strawberries, washed and hulled*
> ¼ *cup cold water*
> ¾ *cup sugar*
> 1½ *tablespoons cornstarch*
> 1 *teaspoon butter*
> 1 *teaspoon lemon juice*
> 4 *drops red food coloring*
> 1 *recipe pastry for double-crust pie (page 119)*
> 1 *3-ounce package cream cheese, softened*
> 1 *tablespoon milk*
> 1 *teaspoon lemon juice*

Set aside ¾ of the berries for the top of the tartlets; crush the remaining berries and place in a small saucepan. Add water, sugar, and cornstarch; stir until cornstarch is completely dissolved. Cook over medium heat, stirring constantly, until mixture begins to boil. Add butter and lemon juice. Add red food coloring. Cool. Roll out pastry to ⅛-inch thickness. Cut out twelve 4-inch circles. Fit into individual tart pans. Place on jelly roll pan for ease in handling. Bake in 400°F. oven for 10 to 15 minutes, or until golden brown. Blend cream cheese, milk, and then lemon juice. Spread on bottom of shells. Fill shells with whole reserved strawberries. Spoon cooled glaze over the strawberries. Chill. Makes 12 tartlets.

HUNGARIAN APPLE SOUR CREAM TARTLETS

> 1 recipe pastry for double-crust pie (page 119)
> 2 cups canned apple slices, drained and coarsely chopped
> ½ cup sugar
> ¼ cup flour
> 3 eggs, well beaten
> 1½ cups dairy sour cream
> 1 teaspoon vanilla
> ¼ cup chopped nuts
> 1 teaspoon ground cinnamon
> 2 tablespoons firmly packed dark brown sugar
> 2 tablespoons butter
> dairy sour cream for garnish (optional)

Prepare pastry and roll out. Use to line bottom and sides of eight 2½-inch deep tart pans. Mix chopped apple slices with sugar, 2 tablespoons of flour, eggs, sour cream, and vanilla. Spoon mixture into tart pans. Mix nuts, remaining 2 tablespoons flour, cinnamon, and brown sugar. Cut in butter until mixture is crumbly. Sprinkle crumbs over top of tarts. Place filled tart pans on a cookie sheet. Bake in a preheated 375°F. oven for 30 to 35 minutes or until filling is firm. Serve warm or cold, with dollops of sour cream if desired. Makes 8 servings.

CHERRY TARTLETS

> ½ cup sugar *
> 2 tablespoons cornstarch
> ½ teaspoon salt
> 1 1-pound can pitted sour cherries, drained with ½ cup juice
>   reserved
> 1 tablespoon butter
> 1 teaspoon lemon juice
> 1 recipe pastry for double-crust pie (page 119)
> 1 3-ounce package cream cheese, softened
> 1 tablespoon milk

* If cherries are packed in heavy syrup, reduce sugar to ⅓ cup.

HUNGARIAN APPLE SOUR CREAM TARTLETS

Blend sugar, cornstarch, and salt in saucepan. Gradually stir in reserved juice from cherries. Cook over medium heat, stirring constantly, until mixture thickens and comes to a full boil. Stir in butter, lemon juice, and drained cherries. Cool. Roll out pastry to ⅛-inch thickness. Cut out twelve 4-inch circles. Fit into individual tart pans. Place on jelly roll pan for ease in handling. Bake in 400°F. oven for 10 to 15 minutes, or until golden brown. Blend cream cheese and milk. Spread in bottom of shells. Fill shells with cherry filling. Makes 12 servings.

Meringues make an easy and interesting base for a tartlet. Here are several with rich-tasting fillings that will make you proud to serve them.

ORANGE MERINGUE TARTLETS

MERINGUE:

3 egg whites
¼ teaspoon cream of tartar
⅛ teaspoon salt
¾ cup sugar

Beat egg whites until foamy; add cream of tartar and salt; beat until stiff, but not dry. Gradually add sugar, beating until very stiff. Cover baking sheet with heavy brown paper or aluminum foil. With spoon or pastry bag, pile meringue into 6 rounds about 3 inches in diameter on covered baking sheet. Make a 2-inch depression in center of each. Bake in 275°F. oven 1 hour. Cool.

ORANGE FILLING:

3 egg yolks
2 tablespons sugar
⅛ teaspoon salt
6 tablespoons frozen orange juice concentrate, thawed, undiluted
1½ teaspoons grated orange rind
1 cup heavy cream, whipped
6 orange sections

Beat egg yolks in top of double boiler. Add sugar, salt, and undiluted orange concentrate. Cook over boiling water, stirring constantly, until thickened. Remove from heat; add orange rind and chill. Fold in whipped cream. Spoon into meringues. Chill 12 to 24 hours. To serve, garnish with orange sections. Makes 6 servings.

ORANGE MERINGUE TARTLETS

CUSTARD MERINGUE TARTLETS

> 1 recipe Meringues (page 207, Orange Meringue Tartlets)
> ¼ cup sugar
> 1 teaspoon flour
> ⅛ teaspoon salt
> 1 cup milk
> 3 egg yolks, beaten
> 1 teaspoon vanilla

Blend sugar, flour, and salt in a heavy saucepan. Add milk. Cook over medium heat, stirring constantly, until bubbly and thickened. Add a small amount of the hot mixture to egg yolks and blend. Return egg yolks to the rest of the mixture in the saucepan and continue cooking for 1 minute more. Remove from heat and cool at once. (Cool by pouring custard into chilled bowl and place in refrigerator or into pan of cold water. Immediate cooling of the custard is important to prevent curdling.) After custard is cooled, blend in vanilla. Chill until serving time. Fill meringue shells with the custard just before serving. Top with Cherry-Cinnamon Sauce on page 67, if desired.

LEMON MERINGUE TARTLETS

> 1 recipe Meringues (page 207, Orange Meringue Tartlets)
> 1¼ cups sugar
> 3 tablespoons cornstarch
> 1¼ cups water
> 3 egg yolks
> 1 whole egg
> 1½ tablespoons butter
> 2 teaspoons grated lemon rind
> ⅓ cup lemon juice

Thoroughly combine sugar and cornstarch in top of a double boiler. Stir in water. Cook over medium heat over water, until mixture boils; reduce heat and cook 1 minute more. Beat egg yolks and egg together. Blend small amount of hot mixture into eggs. Return to hot mixture and blend thoroughly. Place over simmering water and cook, stirring constantly, until thickened. Stir in butter and lemon rind. Gradually stir in lemon juice until well blended. Chill. Spoon into baked meringues and serve. Makes 6 servings.

WALNUT MERINGUE TARTLETS

> 3 egg whites
> 1 teaspoon water
> 1 cup granulated sugar
> ½ cup soda cracker crumbs
> ¾ cup finely chopped walnuts
> 1 teaspoon vanilla

Combine egg whites and water; beat until stiff. Slowly beat in sugar until mixture is very stiff. Gently fold in cracker crumbs, walnuts, and vanilla. Line well greased 3-inch muffin tins with the mixture, building up sides and leaving a depression in middle. Bake shells at 325°F. for 50 to 60 minutes; when done they appear lightly browned, cracked, and dry. Cool shells slightly; then carefully remove from pan. Punch down center slightly to make room for Custard Filling.

> CUSTARD FILLING:
> ½ cup granulated sugar
> 3 tablespoons cornstarch
> 2 cups milk
> 3 egg yolks
> 1 teaspoon vanilla
> 1 tablespoon butter
> 2 teaspoons instant coffee, optional
> 1 cup heavy cream, whipped
> 12 walnut halves

Combine sugar and cornstarch in saucepan; slowly stir in milk. Cook over medium heat, stirring, until mixture comes to a boil and is thickened. Beat egg yolks, stir some of custard into egg yolks; then return to saucepan and cook an additional three minutes. Stir in vanilla, butter, and if desired, instant coffee. Cover and refrigerate until cold. Spoon into meringue shells at least one hour before serving. Top with a swirl of whipped cream and decorate with a walnut half. Makes 12 servings.

LINZER TARTLETS

> 1¾ cups flour
> ½ cup sugar
> ¼ teaspoon cinnamon
> ¼ teaspoon cloves
>   grated rind of 1 lemon
> 2½ cups grated unblanched almonds
> ½ cup cold sweet butter
> 1 egg yolk
> 1 egg white, slightly beaten
> ½ cup sliced almonds
> 2 cups seedless raspberry preserves

Mix flour, sugar, cinnamon, cloves, lemon rind, grated almonds, butter, and egg yolk. Knead quickly into a smooth dough. Roll out on a floured board to ⅛-inch thickness. Cut 36 2½-inch rounds, and 36 2½-inch rounds with a 1-inch hole in the center. Place on ungreased baking sheets. Brush rounds with hole with egg white and sprinkle with sliced almonds. Bake in a preheated 325°F. oven for 15 minutes or until lightly browned. Cool on baking sheets. Spread plain cookies with jam and top with almond-covered cookie rings. Fill center with additional preserves. Makes 3 dozen.

This recipe for tiny jam-filled Viennese Kipferl will produce about 6 dozen two-bite pieces. You'll be surprised at how fast they will disappear.

JAM KIPFERL

> 1 12-ounce package pot cheese
> 3 cups flour
> 1½ cups cold sweet butter
> 1½ cups strawberry or other jam
> 1 egg, slightly beaten

Sieve pot cheese. Add flour and butter and knead quickly until a smooth ball of dough is formed. Wrap and chill dough for 1 hour. Roll out dough, a small amount at a time, to ⅛-inch thickness. Cut dough into 3-inch squares. Place 1 teaspoon jam on each square and roll diagonally from one corner to the opposite corner. Pinch edges together and cut several gashes in top to allow filling to show. Place on greased baking sheets. Brush with egg. Bake in preheated 350°F. oven for 15 minutes or until golden brown. Makes about 6 dozen.

ISCHLER COOKIES

> 1½ cups sifted flour
> ⅓ cup sugar
> 2½ cups finely grated walnuts
> ¾ cup cold sweet butter
> 1 cup strawberry preserves
> 1 6-ounce package semisweet chocolate pieces

Mix flour, sugar, and walnuts. Add butter and knead until smooth and firm. Work quickly to keep butter from melting. Chill dough for 1 hour. Roll out dough on a floured board to ⅛-inch thickness. Cut into 72 2-inch rounds. Place on ungreased cookie sheets and bake in a preheated 350°F. oven for 10 to 15 minutes or until cookies are lightly browned. Cool cookies on cookie sheets. Spread half of the cookies with strawberry preserves. Melt chocolate pieces over hot water. Spread a thin layer of chocolate over remaining cookies. Place chocolate-covered cookie on top of cookies spread with strawberry preserves. Makes 36 cookies.

(Top tier) JEWEL ALMOND TARTLETS, (middle tier) LINZER TARTLETS, ISCHLER COOKIES, (bottom tier) JAM KIPFERL

JEWEL ALMOND TARTLETS

> 1 recipe pastry for double-crust pie (page 119)
> 1 8-ounce package almond paste
> 1 cup sugar
> 3 eggs
> ¼ cup flour
>   assorted preserves: apricot, peach, raspberry, strawberry

Prepare pastry. Cut dough into 36 equal pieces. Press dough evenly into 36 2-inch oval tart pans. Crumble almond paste and mix with sugar. Beat in eggs one at a time until mixture is smooth and creamy. Beat in flour. Fill pastry-lined pans ¾ full. Bake in a preheated 375° F. oven for 15 to 20 minutes or until tarts are richly browned. Cool tarts in pan and then remove. Spread top of each with a thin layer of one of the assorted preserves. Makes 3 dozen.

BLACK LACE WAFERS

> 1 cup sifted flour
> 3 tablespoons cocoa
> 1 cup chopped flaked coconut or finely chopped nuts
> ½ cup light corn syrup
> ½ cup firmly packed granlated sugar
> ½ cup margarine
> 1 teaspoon vanilla

Sift flour with cocoa and mix with coconut or nuts. Combine corn syrup, sugar, and margarine in heavy saucepan. Bring to boil over medium heat, stirring constantly. Remove from heat. Gradually blend in flour-coconut mixture, then stir in vanilla. Drop batter onto foil-covered cookie sheet by scant teaspoonfuls, 3 inches apart. Bake in 350°F. oven 8 to 10 minutes. Cool on wire rack until foil may easily be peeled off, 3 to 4 minutes. Remove foil; cool cookies on wire rack covered with absorbent paper. Makes 4½ dozen (3-inch) cookies.

GINGER LACE WAFERS

>   1 cup sifted flour
> ½ teaspoon ginger
>   1 cup chopped flaked coconut or finely chopped nuts
> ½ cup light or dark corn syrup
> ½ cup firmly packed brown sugar
> ½ cup margarine

Mix sifted flour, ginger, and coconut or nuts. Combine corn syrup, brown sugar, and margarine in heavy saucepan. Bring to boil over medium heat, stirring constantly. Remove from heat. Gradually blend in flour-coconut mixture. Drop batter onto foil-covered cookie sheet by scant teaspoonfuls, 3 inches apart. Bake in 350°F. oven 8 to 10 minutes. Cool on wire rack until foil may easily be peeled off, 3 to 4 minutes. Remove foil; cool cookies on wire rack covered with absorbent paper. Makes 4½ dozen (3-inch) cookies.

FLORENTINES

>   1 cup sifted flour
>   1 cup chopped flaked coconut or finely chopped nuts
> ½ cup light or dark corn syrup
> ½ cup firmly packed brown sugar
> ½ cup margarine
>   1 teaspoon vanilla
>   1 6-ounce package semisweet chocolate chips

Mix sifted flour and coconut or nuts. Combine corn syrup, brown sugar, and margarine in heavy saucepan. Bring to boil over medium heat, stirring constantly. Remove from heat. Gradually blend in flour-coconut mixture, then stir in vanilla. Drop batter by ½ teaspoonfuls onto foil-covered cookie sheet, 3 inches apart. Bake in 350°F. oven 8 to 10 minutes. Cool on wire rack until foil may easily be peeled off, 3 to 4 minutes. Remove foil. Melt semisweet chocolate chips over hot water. Spread melted chocolate on smooth side of one cookie and top with plain cookie, lacy side out. Makes about 50.

PINEAPPLE-CINNAMON REFRIGERATOR COOKIES

½ cup butter
⅓ cup firmly packed light brown sugar
⅓ cup granulated sugar
1 egg
1¾ cups flour
¾ teaspoon baking soda
2 to 3 teaspoons cinnamon
⅓ cup finely chopped nuts
1 teaspoon vanilla

In a small mixing bowl cream butter; gradually add sugars and beat until light and fluffy. Beat in egg. Sift together flour, baking soda, and cinnamon; gradually add to creamed mixture. Blend in nuts and vanilla. Chill for ease in handling. On waxed paper shape into 2 rolls, each 10 inches long and 1¼ inches in diameter. Wrap in waxed paper; chill several hours or overnight. Cut rolls into ⅛-inch slices and place on baking sheet. Bake in a preheated 375°F. oven for 7 to 8 minutes. Remove from baking sheet to wire rack to cool. Frost cookies with Pineapple-Butter Frosting. Makes about 7 dozen.

PINEAPPLE-BUTTER FROSTING:

3 cups confectioners' sugar
¼ cup well-drained crushed pineapple
2 tablespoons butter, softened

In small mixing bowl beat together sugar, pineapple, and butter until smooth.

CHOCOLATE BARS

FIRST LAYER:
½ cup butter
¼ cup sugar
¼ cup cocoa
¼ cup milk
1 egg, slightly beaten
1 teaspoon vanilla
1⅔ cups fine graham cracker crumbs (20 crackers)
1 3½-ounce can flaked coconut
¾ cup finely chopped nuts

In a 2-quart saucepan melt butter. Stir in sugar and cocoa until smooth. Add milk; heat to boiling. Blend a small amount of hot mixture into egg; return all to saucepan. Stir until thickened. Add vanilla. Then stir in crumbs, coconut, and nuts. Press mixture into bottom of an 8-inch buttered square cake pan.

SECOND LAYER:
6 tablespoons butter
1½ cups confectioners' sugar
1 tablespoon milk
1 teaspoon vanilla

In small mixing bowl cream butter and gradually add confectioners' sugar and beat until light and fluffy. Blend in milk and vanilla. Spread over crumb mixture and chill for about 15 minutes.

THIRD LAYER:
1 cup semisweet chocolate pieces
2 tablespoons butter
1½ tablespoons milk
coarsely chopped nuts

In a small saucepan combine chocolate, butter, and milk. Heat over low heat, stirring constantly, until smooth. Spread on chocolate mixture; garnish with nuts; chill. When firm, cut into 1½- by 1-inch pieces. Makes about 30 bars.

ORANGE-FROSTED DATE BARS

> 1 8-ounce package dates, cut up
> ¾ cup firmly packed dark brown sugar
> ½ cup water
> ½ cup butter
> 3 eggs, slightly beaten
> 1½ cups sifted flour
> ¾ teaspoon baking soda
> ½ teaspoon salt
> ½ cup milk
> ½ cup orange juice
> 1 cup chopped unblanched almonds

In a 3-quart saucepan cook dates, brown sugar, and water over low heat, stirring constantly, until dates soften. Remove from heat; add butter; stir until melted. Blend in eggs. Sift together flour, baking soda, and salt; add all at once to date mixture; stir to blend. Gradually stir in milk and orange juice. Stir in nuts. Pour mixture into a buttered 15- by 10- by 1-inch jelly roll pan. Bake in a preheated 350°F. oven for 25 to 30 minutes. Cool in pan on wire rack. Spread Orange Glaze over top and cut into bars to serve. Makes 3 to 4 dozen.

> ORANGE GLAZE:
> 2 tablespoons butter
> 1½ cups confectioners' sugar
> 2 to 3 tablespoons light cream
> 1 to 2 teaspoons grated orange rind

In a small mixing bowl cream butter; gradually beat in confectioners' sugar, cream, and orange rind until of spreading consistency. Makes ⅔ cup.

DREAMY PEANUT-BUTTER BARS

> ¼ cup margarine
> ½ cup chunk-style peanut butter
> 1½ cups firmly packed light brown sugar
> 1½ cups flour
> 2 eggs
> 1 teaspoon vanilla
> ½ teaspoon baking powder
> 1 cup shredded coconut
> 1 6-ounce package semisweet chocolate pieces

Grease 9- by 9- by 2-inch baking pan. Mix margarine and peanut butter until blended. Gradually add ½ cup of the brown sugar, beating until fluffy. Add 1 cup of the flour in 2 additions, beating until blended after each addition. Turn into prepared pan and press evenly over bottom. Bake in 350°F. oven about 10 minutes or until lightly browned. Remove from oven. Meanwhile, beat together eggs, vanilla, and remaining 1 cup brown sugar. Add remaining ½ cup flour and baking powder; beat until well blended. Stir in coconut and chocolate pieces. Spread mixture over hot, partially baked layer in pan. Return to oven and bake 30 minutes or until browned. Cool completely in pan on wire rack. Cut in about 32 2¼- by 1-inch bars.

CRANBERRY BONBONS

> BONBON SHELLS:
> 2 cups semisweet chocolate pieces
> ¼ cup butter
> 6 dozen tea-size paper baking cups (2 inches in diameter
>   at top and 1¾ inches across bottom)

Melt chocolate and butter in saucepan over very low heat. Have ready 24 double baking cups, made double by placing one inside another. Using back of spoon, spread melted chocolate over inside of baking cup to cover completely. Place in refrigerator 30 minutes, until firm. Carefully peel baking cups from chocolate and slip chocolate shells into clean baking cups. Return to refrigerator.

CRANBERRY FILLING:
- 1 *envelope (1 tablespoon) unflavored gelatin*
- ¾ *cup fresh orange juice*
- 1 *pound fresh cranberries*
- 1½ *cups sugar*
- 2 *teaspoons grated orange rind*
- 1 *cup heavy cream*

Sprinkle gelatin over ½ cup orange juice in small saucepan. Place over low heat; stir constantly until gelatin dissolves, about 3 minutes. Remove from heat. Place cranberries in medium saucepan with remaining ¼ cup orange juice, sugar, and orange rind. Cook over medium heat, stirring occasionally, until cranberry skins pop, about 10 minutes. Remove from heat; stir in gelatin mixture. Chill until mixture is completely cooled and slightly thickened. Whip cream; fold into cooled cranberry mixture. Spoon into chilled chocolate shells and refrigerate until set. Makes 24 bonbons.

CRANBERRY BONBONS

BABY APPLE BABAS

Sometimes it is a relief to get a head start with convenience foods while turning out something that looks as though you had spent many more hours in the kitchen. This is a recipe for a moment like that.

BABY APPLE BABAS
(A Quick-trick Way)

> 1 package yellow cake mix
> canned applesauce
> whipped cream, optional

Prepare cake mix according to package directions, substituting canned applesauce for water or milk called for. Spoon the batter into 10 well-greased paper hot-drink cups. Place on baking sheet. Bake in 375°F. oven 30 to 35 minutes, or until done. Cool 5 minutes. Tip cakes out of paper cups. While still warm, drizzle over each cake 1 teaspoon Rum Sauce. Chill. Serve with remaining sauce and whipped cream, if desired. Makes 10 servings.

> RUM SAUCE:
> ¾ cup sugar
> 1 cup apple juice
> 3 tablespoons orange peel, cut in slivers
> 1 tablespoon lemon juice
> 1 teaspoon rum flavoring

Combine sugar, apple juice, orange peel, and lemon juice in small saucepan. Cook and stir over low heat 7 minutes. Remove from heat. Stir in flavoring. Use hot or cold. Makes 1¼ cups of sauce.

PINK FLUFF SQUARES

    ½ cup butter
    ¼ cup firmly packed light brown sugar
 1¼ cups flour
    ¼ cup maraschino cherry juice
    ¼ cup water
    1 envelope (1 tablespoon) unflavored gelatin
 1½ cups sugar
    ½ cup water
    ½ cup chopped maraschino cherries
    ½ cup toasted, chopped, blanched almonds
    1 teaspoon almond extract

In a small mixing bowl cream butter; gradually add brown sugar and beat until light and fluffy. Gradually mix in flour. (Mixture may be crumbly.) Press into bottom of buttered 9-inch square baking pan. Bake in a preheated 325°F. oven for 25 minutes or until golden brown. Cool in pan on wire rack. Combine cherry juice and ¼ cup water; sprinkle gelatin over liquid to soften. In a 1-quart saucepan combine sugar and ½ cup water; bring to boil, stirring constantly, and boil for 2 minutes. Remove from heat. Stir in softened gelatin until gelatin is dissolved. Pour into small mixing bowl and immediately whip at high speed of mixer until quite thick (about 10 minutes). Reserve 1 tablespoon each chopped cherries and almonds for garnish. Fold in remaining cherries, almonds, and almond extract. Spread over cooled cookie layer. Sprinkle reserved cherries and almonds over top. Chill for several hours or overnight. Cut into 1½-inch squares with a moistened knife. (Keep leftovers refrigerated.) Makes 18 pieces.

WALNUT-CHERRY SQUARES

> 1 cup walnuts
> 1¼ cups sifted flour
> ½ cup brown sugar, packed
> ½ cup butter
> ½ cup flaked coconut
> 1 8-ounce package cream cheese
> ⅓ cup granulated sugar
> 1 egg
> 1 teaspoon vanilla
> 1 21-ounce can cherry pie filling

Chop ½ cup walnuts coarsely, and set aside for top of squares. Chop remaining walnuts fine, for bottom layer. Combine flour, brown sugar, and butter and blend to fine crumbs. Add coconut and finely chopped walnuts, and mix well. Set aside ½ cup. Pack remainder into bottom of greased baking pan, 9 by 13 by 2 inches. Bake in a 350°F. oven 12 to 15 minutes, until edges are very lightly browned. Meanwhile, soften cream cheese and beat in ⅓ cup sugar, egg, and vanilla. Continue beating until very smooth. Spread over hot baked layer, and bake 10 minutes longer. Remove from oven and spread cherry pie filling over cheese layer. Sprinkle with the coarsely chopped walnuts and the reserved crumbs. Bake 15 minutes longer. Cool before cutting into squares. Makes 12 3-inch squares.

12

Delectable Crêpes and Soufflés

Preparing crêpes and soufflés well is a true mastery of the simple egg, and one of the high points of culinary art.

A CRÊPE *is a thin pancake made of egg batter and then stuffed or sauced in a gratifying way. Gourmets invariably prefer the famous Crêpes Suzette, with their dazzling flames and lingering flavors. But other crêpes merit attention too, and you will find several unusual combinations in this chapter.*

A SOUFFLÉ *is a puffed-up baked dish, preferably made with a removable collar so that the finished product will rise high above the rim of the baking utensil. It is aerated with stiffly beaten and folded egg whites and will capsize quickly, so it demands last-minute preparation and serving. Because of this handicap to the hostess, several unbaked cold soufflés that have a gelatin base to hold the ingredients intact for many hours are offered in the recipes that follow. One has whipped cream rather than beaten egg whites but is served in a soufflé dish for effect. The choice of soufflé will depend upon the time you can spend in the kitchen just before serving, and whether you prefer a hot or cold dessert. Whatever your choice, do spoon it rather than slice it for best serving results.*

CHOCOLATE CRÊPES

CRÊPES:
¾ cup flour
1 tablespoon sugar
¾ teaspoon salt
3 eggs
¾ cup milk
¼ cup melted butter
   additional butter

Sift together flour, sugar, and salt. Beat eggs well. Add milk, melted butter, and flour mixture; beat until smooth. Cover and refrigerate 1 hour. If batter thickens, add a little milk to return to original thin cream consistency. To prepare crêpes, heat about ½ teaspoon butter in a small, 8-inch skillet, tipping and swirling pan to coat bottom and sides. Add about 2 tablespoons of batter and tip and tilt the pan so that the batter will flow in a thin film over the bottom of pan. When lightly browned, turn and brown other side. Stack crêpes between paper towels until ready to fill.

CHOCOLATE FILLING:
1 cup dairy sour cream
2 tablespoons shaved semisweet chocolate
¼ cup butter
2 tablespoons sugar
½ cup crème de cacao

Combine sour cream and 1 tablespoon of the shaved chocolate. Place about 1 tablespoon of the sour cream mixture in the center of each crêpe; fold in quarters. In crêpe pan, over direct flame, heat butter and sugar until sugar dissolves. Add crêpes and pour crème de cacao over them; heat. Apply lighted match to heated liqueur to flame; shake pan until flames die. Sprinkle remaining tablespoon shaved chocolate over crêpes. Makes 6 servings of 2 crêpes each.

If you plan to flambé this crêpe dessert at the table, you will capture your guests' attention and create a little excitement about dessert. Do have the crêpes prepared ahead of time, and the rest of the ingredients arranged so the performance will go smoothly.

LIME-STRAWBERRY CRÊPES

CRÊPES:
- ⅔ cup sifted flour
- 1 tablespoon sugar
- ½ teaspoon salt
- 3 whole eggs
- 3 egg yolks
- 1½ cups milk
- 2 tablespoons butter, melted
- 1 tablespoon brandy
  additional butter

Sift together flour, sugar, and salt. In a bowl, beat the whole eggs and egg yolks well; add milk. Stir in flour mixture, butter, and brandy; beat until smooth. Cover and refrigerate for 2 hours. To prepare crêpes, heat about ½ teaspoon butter in a small 8-inch skillet, tipping and swirling pan to coat bottom and sides. Add several tablespoons of batter and tip and tilt the pan so that the batter will flow in a thin film over the bottom of pan. When lightly browned, turn and brown other side. Stack crêpes between paper towels or waxed paper until ready to fill.

LIME-STRAWBERRY FILLING:
- 1 quart strawberries, washed, hulled, and halved
- ¼ cup butter
- ½ cup brown sugar
- ⅓ cup lime juice
- ½ cup orange liqueur
- 1 cup heavy cream, whipped
- 1 teaspoon grated lime rind

Place about 6 strawberry halves in a row in the center of each crêpe; roll

LIME-STRAWBERRY CRÊPES

up crêpes and set aside. In crêpe pan, over direct flame, heat butter. Stir in sugar. Add lime juice, stirring constantly; bring to a boil and simmer for 2 minutes. Add crêpes and heat, basting with sauce. Sprinkle crêpes with orange liqueur; apply lighted match and flame. Shake pan until flames burn out. Serve with whipped cream dollops and sprinkle with lime rind. Makes 12 servings.

*Escorted by Niels Olsen, the dynamic young promotion man-
ager of the new Hotel Scandinavia in Copenhagen, I was
pleased to observe a session of the retaurant industry's Lærlin-
geskole, where Danish chefs receive their expert training.
Gert Sørensen, a chef-pàtissier, lecturer, and author, was
teaching the class how to prepare Crêpes Suzette. Afterward
we all had a taste—it certainly had the master's touch!*

CRÊPES SUZETTE

CRÊPES:
- ¾ cup flour
- 6 eggs
- 6 tablespoons butter, melted
- 2¼ cups light cream
- 1 tablespoon sugar
- ½ teaspoon salt
- 1 teaspoon grated lemon rind
- oil for frying

Mix the flour with the eggs. Pour in hot melted butter. Add cream, sugar, salt, and grated lemon rind. Brush an 8-inch skillet with oil, heat the skillet, and fill with a few tablespoons of batter, turning and twisting the pan so that the batter forms a thin coating. When it is browned on one side, turn and brown the other, then remove from the pan and fold in quarters so that the crêpe has a triangular shape. Repeat until all the batter is used, placing each crêpe on a plate over hot water, overlapping as you make the crêpes. When you have made the crêpes, make the sauce and serve. Makes about 30 crêpes; serve 3 to each portion.

SAUCE:
- juice of 2 oranges
- orange rind, shredded
- ¾ cup sugar
- ½ cup butter
- ¼ cup brandy
- ¼ cup curaçao

Place the juice, rind, sugar, and butter in a flambè pan. Cook gently as you stir until rind is softened. Add brandy and curaçao. Swirl each crêpe through the sauce and place overlapped to one side, until they have all been treated this way. With a spatula, spread the crêpes over the entire pan. Then pour extra warmed brandy over the top, ignite, and shake the pan until the flames die down. Serve at once.

MOLASSES-ORANGE CRÊPES

CRÊPES:
- ¾ cup sifted flour
- ¾ teaspoon salt
- 3 eggs
- 1 cup milk
- 1½ tablespoons butter, melted
- 1 tablespoon grated orange rind

Combine flour and salt. Beat eggs; stir in milk and butter. Stir in flour mixture and grated orange rind. For each crêpe, pour several tablespoons of batter into a hot greased, 8-inch skillet; tilt to spread thinly. When lightly browned, turn to brown other side. Remove; roll up jelly-roll fashion at once. Place in Molasses-Orange Sauce. Makes 6 servings.

MOLASSES-ORANGE SAUCE:
- 1 6-ounce can frozen orange juice concentrate, thawed, undiluted
- ¼ cup sugar
- ½ cup unsulphured molasses
- ¼ cup butter

Mix together undiluted orange juice concentrate, sugar, molasses, and butter. Heat in chafing dish over open flame, stirring occasionally, until butter is melted and sauce is hot. Place prepared rolled crêpes in the sauce; spoon sauce over. Heat through a moment and serve.

ORANGE CRÊPES

CRÊPES:
3 eggs
2 egg yolks
½ cup milk
½ cup orange juice
  fine salad oil
1 cup flour
¾ teaspoon salt
1 tablespoon sugar
1 tablespoon grated orange rind

Beat eggs and egg yolks. Add milk, orange juice, and salad oil. Stir in flour, salt, sugar, and orange rind. Beat until smooth. Let stand at room temperature for 1 hour. Lightly brush hot 8-inch skillet with salad oil. Add about 2 tablespoons of batter to skillet; turn and tip skillet so that mixture covers bottom evenly. Batter will set immediately into a thin lacy pancake. When it browns, in about 15 to 20 seconds, loosen with a spatula and flip over. Brown other side in just a few seconds and turn crêpe out onto wax paper or foil. Makes 6 servings, of 3 crêpes each.

ORANGE SAUCE:
½ cup soft butter
½ cup confectioners' sugar
1 tablespoon grated orange rind
3 tablespoons orange liqueur (Grand Marnier or Cointreau)
½ cup orange juice
1 cup orange sections

Cream soft butter with confectioners' sugar and orange rind. Gradually blend in orange liqueur. Spread about ½ teaspoon of mixture over side of crêpe that was browned last, as this is the less attractive side. Roll up crêpes with orange mixture inside. Place remaining mixture with orange juice in blazer or crêpe pan over direct flame. Heat until bubbly. Add rolled crêpes and heat, spooning sauce over. Add orange sections and heat 2 or 3 minutes more. Serve at once.

It was well worth the trouble to locate the restaurant Mesón de San Javier in the old part of Madrid. It is housed in an ancient building rich with Spanish history, where Chef Denis, the owner, takes pride in the presentation of marvelous cuisine. He brought this recipe with him from a famous restaurant he owned in South America, and prepared it expertly for us at tableside. The flavors combine to give toothsome delight.

CREPES BUENOS AIRES

      6 dessert crêpes (use recipe on page 229)
      ¼ cup Cointreau liqueur
      ¼ cup rum
      1 teaspoon sugar
      1 tablespoon butter
      1 tablespoon butterscotch sauce
      1 teaspoon raspberry jam
      2 tablespoons whipped cream
      1 tablespoon chopped walnuts

Prepare dessert crêpes as directed and set aside. (This may be done ahead of time. Stack crêpes between waxed paper and refrigerate until needed.) Combine Cointreau, rum, sugar, and butter in a skillet or flambé pan; simmer for about 5 minutes, stirring occasionally to blend. Meanwhile, combine butterscotch sauce, raspberry jam, whipped cream, and walnuts. Spread crêpes with this whipped cream mixture and roll up; place in skillet and spoon sauce over all. Serve at once. Makes 6 servings.

*The Three Hussars Restaurant, considered to be the finest
dining room in Vienna, serves fresh strawberries, chocolate
sauce, and whipped cream over several round pancakes—instead of as a filling for a crêpe. Either way, it has to be tasted
to be believed.*

AUSTRIAN SPRINGTIME CRÊPES

    1 cup milk
    2 eggs
       pinch of salt
    ¼ cup carbonated water, still bubbling
    1 cup sifted flour
       butter, melted
    1 quart fresh strawberries, hulled and washed
    1 cup prepared chocolate fudge sauce
       whipped cream

Combine milk and eggs; add salt. Beat in carbonated water. Stir in flour.
Heat in 8-inch skillet and brush with melted butter. Spoon in just
enough batter to coat bottom of pan. Cook for several minutes, until
lightly browned; then turn and lightly brown other side. Remove to a
warm place and repeat process until batter is used up. Fill each crêpe
with fresh strawberries; spoon chocolate sauce over top, and garnish with
dollops of whipped cream. Makes about 12 crêpes.

GRAPE SOUFFLÉ

    ¾ cup Concord grape jelly
    2 teaspoons lemon juice
    3 egg whites
    ⅛ teaspoon cream of tartar
    ⅛ teaspoon salt
    3 tablespoons sugar

Heat the jelly in a saucepan until melted, then stir in lemon juice, and
cool. Beat egg whites with the cream of tartar and salt, until soft peaks

form; then gradually add sugar while beating, until whites are stiff. Fold jelly through egg whites very gently. Pour into a 6-cup soufflé dish and bake in a 350°F. oven for 20 to 25 minutes. Makes 4 to 6 servings.

While in Paris recently, I watched Cordon Bleu's chef-professeur, Charles Narsès, demonstrate this dessert soufflé. His audience gasped with pleasure as he skillfully shaped this free-form version and then decorated it with more of the mixture in a pastry bag. Then after a quick trip to a hot oven, the soufflé emerged lightly browned and holding its precarious shape. Truly a master artist at work.

CORDON BLEU DESSERT SOUFFLÉ

    3 eggs, separated
    ½ cup sugar
    1 teaspoon vanilla
       confectioners' sugar

Beat egg yolks until light and frothy; then gradually add sugar and beat fast and well until mixture thickens. Add vanilla. In a separate bowl, beat egg whites until stiff. Fold the two mixtures together, being careful not to break down the air bubbles. Spoon about ½ cup of the mixture into a pastry bag, if decorating is desired. Quickly spoon the remaining mixture into an oval-shaped mound on a flat baking and serving tray; run a spatula around the side to make scalloped indentations. Then decorate the edges and surface with reserved mixture in the pastry bag, if you have chosen to do so. Sift a light dusting of confectioners' sugar over all. Put at once into a preheated 425°F. oven for 4 to 5 minutes, or until lightly browned. Turn oven off; open oven door slightly for several moments. Then remove soufflé and serve at once. Makes 6 servings.

If you never serve a dessert soufflé because you fear it may fall, serve a chilled soufflé that can be made ahead to wait in the refrigerator until time for dessert. To make the collar for the soufflé, fold foil into four thicknesses 3 inches wide and long enough to go around the dish with a generous overlap. Attach it to a soufflé dish with sealing tape, leaving 1 inch of the foil around the dish to make a collar 2 inches high. After chilling the soufflé, remove the foil collar at serving time, and spoon out the fluffy mixture.

STRAWBERRY SOUFFLÉ

    2 *envelopes (2 tablespoons) unflavored gelatin*
    1 *cup milk*
    2 *10-ounce packages frozen strawberries, thawed*
    6 *egg whites*
  ¼ *teaspoon salt*
  ½ *cup sugar*
    2 *cups heavy cream*

Sprinkle gelatin over milk in medium saucepan; let stand until gelatin is moistened. Place over low heat; stir constantly until gelatin dissolves, about 5 minutes. Remove from heat; stir in strawberries. Beat egg whites with salt in large bowl until stiff but not dry. Gradually add sugar and beat until very stiff. Fold in strawberry mixture. Whip cream and fold in. Turn into soufflé dish that measures 2½ quarts to the rim, with a 2-inch collar. Chill until firm. Remove collar. If desired, garnish soufflé with additional whipped cream. Makes 8 servings.

STRAWBERRY SOUFFLÉ

APPLESAUCE FROZEN SOUFFLÉ JUBILEE

> 2 *15-ounce jars applesauce*
> ½ *teaspoon cinnamon*
> 1½ *cups heavy cream*
> 1 *14½-ounce jar pitted dark sweet cherries*
> 1 *teaspoon cornstarch*

Combine applesauce and cinnamon. Whip cream until stiff; fold into applesauce. Pour mixture into 4-cup collared soufflé dish. (Or use 5-cup serving dish.) Freeze until firm, several hours or overnight. Drain juice from cherries and heat with cornstarch, stirring occasionally, until it comes to a boil and thickens. Carefully remove collar from frozen soufflé and decorate top with cherries. Add remaining cherries to thickened juice and serve as a sauce with the soufflé. Makes 8 to 10 servings.

BRANDY ALEXANDER SOUFFLÉ
(A Diet Dessert)

> 1 *envelope (1 tablespoon) unflavored gelatin*
> 1 *cup skimmed milk, divided*
> 4 *eggs, separated*
>   *nonnutritive sweetener equivalent to ⅓ cup sugar*
> ⅛ *teaspoon salt*
> 2 *tablespoons brandy*
> 2 *tablespoons crème de cacao*
> ⅓ *cup sugar*
>   *green grapes, optional*
>   *mint sprigs, optional*

Soften gelatin in ½ cup cold milk in top of double boiler. In bowl, beat together egg yolks and remaining ½ cup milk. Add to gelatin mixture. Place over boiling water and cook, stirring constantly, until gelatin dissolves and mixture thickens slightly, about 5 minutes. Remove from heat; stir in nonnutritive sweetener, salt, brandy, and crème de cacao. Chill, stirring occasionally, until mixture mounds slightly when dropped from a spoon. Beat egg whites until stiff, but not dry; gradually add sugar and beat until very stiff. Fold into gelatin mixture. Turn into 4-cup soufflé dish and chill several hours, until set. If desired, garnish with green grapes and mint sprigs. Makes 8 (½ cup) servings, 115 calories per serving.

You haven't had the best Fettucine Alfredo until you've had it in Rome, with the maestro himself wielding the golden spoon and fork to toss the fresh noodles and cheese. But you can easily duplicate Alfredo's special Omelet Flambé with these directions from Chef Peter Di Napoli. Small oval baking dishes, one for each person, are a must to do it right. A perfect dessert for a salad luncheon!

OMELET FLAMBÉ ALFREDO

FOR EACH OMELET:

1 egg, beaten
 butter
2 tablespoons apricot jam, warmed
2 tablespoons sugar
3 ounces rum

Pour beaten egg into a lightly buttered 8-inch omelet pan; cook until just solidified. Turn out and spoon jam on the middle; roll up and place in a hot oval buttered baking dish. Spoon sugar over top. Keep on a warming tray until all omelets are made. Then pour rum over each one and set afire. Serve at once, when flames die out.

Vocabulary of Dessert Directions

BAKE: Place in the oven to cook with indirect dry heat; 250°F. is low heat, 350°F. is medium heat, and 450°F. is high heat.

BEAT: Stir food together with a fast movement until completely blended and smooth and slightly aerated.

BLANCH: Dip in boiling water and then in ice water to remove the skins from fruits and nuts.

BLEND: Stir ingredients together until there is a single identity. A circular motion will do.

BOIL: Bring a liquid to the bubbling stage over heat.

CANDY: Glaze with a sugary mixture.

CARAMELIZE: Heat sugar until it melts and browns.

CREAM: Mix fat until it is fluffy.

CUT: With a pastry cutter or a knife in each hand, work fat into flour, until the mixture is of a uniformly mealy texture.

DUST: Sprinkle food lightly with sugar or flour to cover with a light film.

FLAMBÉ: Set food ablaze with alcoholic beverage, then shake it to put the flames out.

FOLD: Use an under-over motion to combine batters without destroying air bubbles.

GLAZE: Cover food with a substance that will cause a shiny surface.

GRATE: Rub food against a surface that will reduce it to smaller particles.

GRIND: Reduce food to tiny particles.

KNEAD: Fold and stretch dough until it becomes smooth and elastic to the touch.

MIX: Stir foods together until combined.

MOLD: Shape food with a container until it will hold a similar shape by itself.

PARE: Cut the skin off, as with fruits.
PEEL: Remove skin by hand, such as banana and orange skin.
POACH: Cook in simmering liquid over low heat.
PURÉE: Reduce food to a smooth sauce in a blender or food mill.
REDUCE: Boil liquid down to a lesser amount and more intense taste.
SIMMER: Cook over very low heat just below the boiling level.
SLIVER: Cut food in long slender pieces.
STIR: Combine ingredients with a slow motion to avoid adding air.
WHIP: Beat ingredients vigorously to add much air and inflate the volume
    of the mixture.

Table of Weights and Measures

AMOUNT	EQUIVALENT
⅓ of ½ teaspoon	A pinch
½ of ¼ teaspoon	⅛ teaspoon
3 teaspoons	1 tablespoon
2 tablespoons	⅛ cup
4 tablespoons	¼ cup
5 tablespoons plus 1 teaspoon	⅓ cup
8 tablespoons	½ cup
10 tablespoons plus 2 teaspoons	⅔ cup
12 tablespoons	¾ cup
16 tablespoons	1 cup
1 cup	8 fluid ounces
2 cups	1 pint
2 pints	1 quart
4 cups	1 quart
2 quarts	½ gallon
4 quarts	1 gallon
16 ounces, dry measure	1 pound
32 ounces, fluid measure	1 quart
¼ pound butter	½ cup
3 ounces cream cheese	6 tablespoons
1 pound flour	4 cups sifted
1 pound cake flour	4¾ cups sifted
1 medium lemon	3 tablespoons juice
1 medium lemon rind	1 tablespoon grated rind
1 medium orange	⅓ cup juice
1 medium orange rind	2 tablespoons grated rind
1 pound unshelled walnuts	1⅔ cups chopped walnuts
1 pound granulated sugar	2½ cups
1 pound brown sugar	2⅛ cups
1 pound confectioners' sugar	3½ cups
1 cup raw rice	3 cups cooked rice

Index

INDEX